ADVANCE PRAISE

"With this book, Harry Clark has given aspiring entrepreneurs a magnificent gift. By sharing stories of business failures and lessons learned from thirty entrepreneurs who made fortunes—and then lost it all—he offers invaluable advice. Don't make the same mistakes: Learn from theirs!"

> —*Harvey Mackay*, author of the #1 *New York Times* bestseller
> *Swim with the Sharks Without Being Eaten Alive*

"For over thirty years I have represented numerous successful business people and high net worth individuals in financial crisis, including at least one identified in *Mistakes Millionaires Make*. Frequently, clients have said, 'I'm going to write a book when this is over.' Now someone has. Harry Clark has collected and distilled the experiences and lessons learned by thirty such individuals. It is a work unlike any other. I wholeheartedly recommend it to my friends, colleagues, and clients, including those I have not yet met."

> —*Dale Schian*, Bankruptcy Attorney, Schian Walker, PLC

"Harry Clark's book is riveting, harrowing, and well written. I want to give copies to my key executives, YPO forum members, board, and family."

> —*Pete Douglas*, PE, President, Douglas Company

"Acquisitions can be an entrepreneur's best friend or biggest mistake. Harry's book speaks to the importance of taking the emotion out of the M&A world and approaching it with the proper due diligence that balances risks with opportunities. Business leaders understand learning from past mistakes can be a valuable lesson in assuring future success. *Mistakes Millionaires Make* supercharges this learning curve in a quick and fun read that pays back tenfold."

—*Mike Dowse*, President, Wilson Sporting Goods

"There is nothing more valuable to business leaders than the insights that come from hard-fought and direct experiences of peers. Drawing from his own challenges and many valuable lessons derived from the unparalleled CEO network of YPO, Harry Clark gives leaders an invaluable roadmap of how to save their own futures from potential losses and all-too-common mistakes. I would recommend this book for any entrepreneur or seasoned executive seeking to strengthen their perspective about success and the risks that come with it."

—*McKeel Hagerty*, CEO of Hagerty Insurance
and International Chair of YPO

"The autographed copy is now a very special part of the LaunchPad library. I especially appreciated how relatable the stories were—inspired ideas for what to avoid and what to do. A great combination of practical plus strategic ideas, and the narrative style makes the lessons stick."

—*Andrea Kates*, CEO, LaunchPad Central

"*Mistakes Millionaires Make* provides an insightful glimpse of the goblins that reside under every entrepreneur's bed—keep the night light on!"

—*Bert Vivian*, former Co-CEO, P.F. Chang's

MISTAKES
MILLIONAIRES
MAKE

LESSONS FROM
30 SUCCESSFUL ENTREPRENEURS

HARRY CLARK

GREENLEAF
BOOK GROUP PRESS

Published by Greenleaf Book Group Press
Austin, Texas
www.gbgpress.com

Distributed by Greenleaf Book Group

For ordering information or special discounts for bulk purchases, please contact Greenleaf Book Group at PO Box 91869, Austin, TX 78709, 512.891.6100.

Design and composition by Greenleaf Book Group
Cover design by Greenleaf Book Group
Interior design by Adina Cucicov

Cataloging-in-Publication Data is available.

Print ISBN: 978-1-62634-328-3

eBook ISBN: 978-1-62634-329-0

TreeNeutral

Part of the Tree Neutral® program, which offsets the number of trees consumed in the production and printing of this book by taking proactive steps, such as planting trees in direct proportion to the number of trees used: www.treeneutral.com

Printed in the United States of America on acid-free paper

16 17 18 19 20 21   10 9 8 7 6 5 4 3 2 1

First Edition

I received significant encouragement from friends and family to develop this body of work. I think they understood the importance of creating something positive from the pain and loss associated with losing my business and my fortune. I want to dedicate this book to my mother, Joyce Clark, who passed away after I had written a draft but before publication. She was always my greatest supporter. I also want to thank my father, who has always been my role model, mentor, and friend. Finally, I want to thank my wife, Heather, and her father, Rich Post, who have listened to me talk about this project for two years. They were patient advisors and sounding boards.

CONTENTS

AUTHOR'S NOTE

This book probably isn't like others you've read. First of all, the entrepreneurs who were interviewed for this book told their stories in the first person, while I recorded them. The style is conversational, and I wanted their authentic voices to be heard.

The other issue is a legal one: Every entrepreneur you will meet in this book had his share of ups and downs and made both great decisions and horrible mistakes. In many cases, external forces had a tremendous impact on them. The specific entities, businesses, and individuals they talk about are part of their stories, and criticism of these entities or people are their opinions, not mine.

The inclusion of names or discussions of people or businesses in this book is in no way an endorsement or a warning about those people or businesses.

Finally, an intended result of this book is to create a heightened awareness for investors, entrepreneurs and family business owners of the risks associated with business and the need to protect themselves, their families and other stakeholders. I encourage the use of the Entrepreneurial Risk Assessment (ERA) to learn more about your individual risk exposure. This 12-minute 50-question self-assessment is available at:

www.ERArisksurvey.com

ACKNOWLEDGMENTS

I want to thank the Young Presidents Organization (YPO), which provides access to unique educational and networking experiences designed to support business, community, and personal leadership to more than 22,000 peers and their families in more than 125 countries. In August 2013 I posted a small request for volunteers to be "victims" of recorded interviews for the research for this book. I specifically asked for entrepreneurs who had made huge fortunes but lost them later and were willing to tell me their stories. Within an hour, I had more than ten responses; within two days, I had been inundated with volunteers or people interested in learning more and participating in the research.

A fundamental value of YPO is trust and confidentiality. Almost all of the thirty entrepreneurs I interviewed allowed me to use their material without caveats. Only two needed to maintain anonymity due to ongoing legal issues.

Without openness and trust, this important research could not be possible. I want to thank each of the members who assisted me in this endeavor, including the following people:

Alejandro Rivas Micoud
Andrew Dumke
Bob Verdun

Brad Adams
Dan Leigh
Dan Stephenson
Don Hannah
Doug Harrison
Gary Greenberg
Jim Glazer
Jim Warner
John Couzens
Matt Hagen
Michael Koffler
Mike Brown
Mike McKeough
Patrick van den Bossche
Peter Bowe
Scott Dickman
Wayne Lee

There are many other people who helped me develop an initial version of this book and collateral material. The team includes Rich Post, Brett Wilson, and Brian Phillips (cover design), LeeAnne Clark, Mercy Pinkerton, Joan Tapper, and Sally Garland (editors), Adina Cucicov (interior design), Jen Glynn (Project Manager), Luis Manuel Ortiz (Spanish translation), and Alex Wibe (analysis for the Entrepreneurial Risk Assessment Survey). Without their help, this book would not have been possible.

PART ONE

INTRODUCTION

There has never been comprehensive research probing common ways that entrepreneurs lose it all. No materials are available to educate entrepreneurs about business pitfalls. There are no college textbooks, classes, workshops, or business books.

To date, the only individuals who seem to have learned these hard lessons are unlucky folks who have fallen off the edge and been wiped out. This book is a compilation of what thirty entrepreneurs—and I, myself—learned along the way.

I conducted interviews with these entrepreneurs, who told me how they had made millions and then lost everything. Many of these individuals remade their fortunes within a few years. A few of their stories brought tears to my eyes, while others left me in disbelief.

Readers need to understand why this book is important to me. So it begins with my story—twenty-five years in the making but only pages in the telling. The remaining chapters recount the stories of the highly successful entrepreneurs who also fell into the abyss. My hope is that I can prevent hundreds of entrepreneurs, aspiring entrepreneurs, and students of entrepreneurship from making the same mistakes. Or, for those who already have undergone business reverses, perhaps it will help to know that others have survived and gone on to prosper.

Entrepreneurs face numerous risks, not just one, and they are covered in this book's various chapters and sections. Each chapter stands on its own; there is no continuing plot in these pages. So I encourage you to consider reading the chapters that are most relevant to you first.

It is my hope that the wisdom gained from this research will help entrepreneurs identify their blind spots and motivate them to make changes in their strategic plans, staffing, financial structures, estate plans, and insurance policies—not just in their businesses but also in their personal lives. I also hope that CEOs will share this book with members of their leadership teams as well as with family, friends, and other stakeholders in the welfare of their companies. It is essential that entrepreneurs surround themselves with those who understand the risks that CEOs face and who can help safeguard them against those risks.

Finally, I hope readers find motivation, perseverance, and hope in these stories of entrepreneurs who lost everything and then gained it all back.

CHAPTER I

FALLING OFF THE CLIFF— MY STORY

"The more assets an estate has,
the more the fight turns into a feeding
frenzy for the attorneys."

This chapter begins my story—how I started and grew two successful Inc. 500 companies, then made the mistakes that cost me $100 million and a decade of agony.

I thought I had it made. I *thought* I had done everything a highly successful entrepreneur needed to do to escape falling off the edge and losing everything. I had a business degree and an MBA from California State University, Long Beach. I had completed countless hours of continuing education every year, and I had what I thought was a comprehensive estate plan with millions of dollars in the bank. I lost it all: my wife of twenty years, $100 million of hard-earned wealth, and a track record of success after success.

I am the youngest of four kids and was raised in New England and California. We moved around often because my father was making his way up the ladder in corporate America. He ended up as CEO and chairman of several multinational computer or technology-distribution companies, some of which were on the New York Stock Exchange. An atmosphere of competition, hard work, long workweeks, and business conversations were a normal part of family life when I was growing up. I started working at age fifteen—I was able to obtain a motorcycle license to drive to my job—and I also wrestled all the way through graduate school as a Division I NCAA heavyweight. School was hard work, but I loved learning.

After I finished my MBA, Deloitte hired me as a staff consultant in the San Diego office. The other junior consultants at Deloitte and I would compete to bill the most hours to our clients. That started a pattern of sixty- to one-hundred-hour workweeks. I believed in the concept of work hard, play hard. And I met Linda, who was also a consultant at Deloitte. She and I were married six months later.

MUNIFINANCIAL

In 1989, when I was twenty-seven, I started my own company, MuniFinancial. I had gotten some much-needed counseling from my dad and an older brother, Jim, who initially was a partner in the business. Jim provided some software development and $25,000 in capital to fund the start-up. In six months the company was launched and profitable. After about a year I bought out my brother's shares and owned all of the company.

MuniFinancial started as a software company to help cities and counties in California manage debt financings. Almost immediately, the clients asked me to actually manage the financings for them rather than just sell them software. At that point, MuniFinancial morphed into what became the largest service provider of municipal debt management in the United States. Within six years the company was involved with about 1,500 bond issues in twenty-six states, with seven offices nationally.

MuniFinancial was making about $1 million a year in profit on income that was steady and highly predictable. This allowed me to buy a beautiful office building, a second home, classic cars, and a collection of fine art. My wife and I also built a house on a large estate on which to raise our daughters. The income enabled us to become involved in various philanthropic causes.

Entrepreneurs know that ownership is ripe with challenges. I also lacked experience—not unusual for someone in his mid-twenties or early thirties. I made plenty of mistakes along the way, but my success made me arrogant and cocky. It truly seemed as though everything I touched turned to gold. Or so I thought.

By 1996 I had sold MuniFinancial to MBIA, Inc., a Fortune 100 financial services company headquartered in Armonk, New York, for a package worth more than $10 million.

After the sale I stayed with MBIA for two years, helping them with a roll-up strategy for municipal services that they abandoned after a year. I spent the second year helping MBIA divest its subsidiaries while I looked for my next business opportunity. My overall goal was to find a niche where I could "do good and do well." I wanted to have a business that could explode with opportunity but also help the world be a better place. I must have looked at a dozen potential new enterprises before finding one that seemed to fit the bill.

TURNKEY

All through the 1990s California continued to fall behind in the quality of its K–12 public school performance and facilities. It was common to drive past a public school campus and see classrooms housed in cheap portable trailers. Partly due to the possibility of earthquakes and the need for schools to be safe, the process of getting a school facility approved and built was extremely costly and time consuming. It would commonly take five or more years to design and construct a simple elementary school campus, and it would cost far more than anyone had imagined. In this inefficiency I saw an opportunity to better the world and make a lot of money.

The business idea behind TurnKey was to make the development of schools faster, more affordable, and of absolutely the highest quality. There were five of us founders, each with our own expertise, but we shared a common vision to improve the process of building schools. My role was to help capitalize the company and act as CEO. We literally started with a clean whiteboard and devoted a weekend to developing a business model to design and build schools in half the time and for 20 percent less than normal. We combined component-based CAD designs (think Legos), modular all-steel construction, "green" architecture, and the latest in educational theory.

We started operations in 1999 and finished our first year of business by securing a few contracts, hiring a few key people, and developing basic systems. By 2000 we had built our first school and had another on the way. We were making all sorts of mistakes by building a business that was far too complex, but the demand for what we were offering was enormous.

SKYROCKETING GROWTH

Our sales by 2002 were $25 million. A year later we had doubled that. We were working like mad to develop the infrastructure necessary to manage this wild growth while at the same time adding more services and functions and therefore making our complex business even more complex.

In 2003 we also opened our own off-site construction plant. We had designed and built it ourselves—almost 100,000 square feet on fourteen acres and very impressive to see. Truly it was the best plant anywhere. We implemented as many cutting-edge innovations as possible and set the industry on its ear. In the same year TurnKey also acquired an electrical contracting company that became the basis of the on-site construction crews. This was far too much expansion in one year. Although the employees found the environment at TurnKey exhilarating, they were highly stressed.

Nevertheless, TurnKey continued to expand. Our run rate for sales was on track for $100 million in 2004 and for more than $200 million for 2005, and we had 450 employees. The sky seemed to be the limit.

CHAPTER 2

HOW THINGS GOT WORSE

*"When times are good, entrepreneurs often feel
like their clients are partners."*

The TurnKey debacle and its collateral damage, which I detail in this chapter, extended far beyond what was ever taught in business school. Some of what occurred seems impossible, but, as we all know, reality is stranger than fiction.

A CLIENT "PARTNERSHIP"

While TurnKey was expanding, a relationship with one of the company's clients started to deteriorate, which contributed greatly to our financial problems. When times are good, entrepreneurs often feel like their clients are partners. In this case, though, when things went bad, our school district "partner" used TurnKey as a scapegoat.

In 2002 the sales team at TurnKey met with representatives of a school district in Santa Barbara County. Their facilities were in terrible shape, with the highest percentage of students in inferior "temporary" classrooms, more than any other district in the state.

The district badly needed several additional new schools, but none had been built since the 1980s. Not only were there no financial resources to construct the buildings, the district had no human expertise to do so. It only knew how to install more portable classrooms.

The district hired TurnKey to build its first new school at lightning speed and for a significant savings. It took just a year and a half of design, approval, and construction, and the district loved it.

Complicating the situation, however, was the fact that the lack of new schools had affected the educational schedule. In late 2002 I attended a meeting in Sacramento about school funding in which the district's superintendent testified that the district would "never be able to get off multi-track year-round schooling because of its hardship and huge shortfall of facilities."

This meant that schools would operate year-round without traditional breaks and vacations, making the best use of limited facilities but imposing difficulties on the community, since, invariably, families have children on different "tracks" whose schedules and breaks seldom coincide.

After he testified, I asked the supervisor if he would be interested in a proposal for us to help the district obtain funding and build enough new schools to return them forever to traditional schedules. The answer was a resounding yes!

A couple of months later, at the end of 2002, the district hired TurnKey to plan, retain funding for, design, and build about eight new schools with a total value of $85 million. The district would be able to remove nearly all of the portable classrooms and eliminate the multi-track, year-round schedules. This was exactly what we were in business for: doing good for the client and its community.

IGNORING STANDARD OPERATING PROCEDURE

Unfortunately, there was a difficult new deadline. California planned to remove the district from its special "hardship status" as of October 2003, and TurnKey had to meet that date with all of the plans, or the district would lose $35 million of the $85 million in state funding for the new projects. Without that money, the district would be unable to build enough new facilities.

Both TurnKey and the district understood that actually preparing all the plans and gaining approval before the deadline was likely impossible, but we agreed to do the best we could. TurnKey design teams worked tirelessly to complete everything in less than half the normal time, although that meant departing from standard business processes. In the end, TurnKey made the deadline and secured the $85 million, an amazing accomplishment.

However, although the plans for the projects were sufficiently detailed for funding approval by the state, they were not finished enough for construction. TurnKey wanted to spend six more months to "clean up" and complete the plans, then bid them out in May or June 2004. The school facilities would be built by June 2005—plenty of time for the opening of school in August of that year.

By October 2003, however, the district had learned that the state would no longer pay districts an increased operating budget allocation if they were on a year-round schedule, starting with the 2004–05 school year. The superintendent said it was imperative that the new schools open by August 2004 to save the district several million dollars. TurnKey reluctantly agreed, with the understanding that the district and TurnKey were partners. So far, TurnKey had always come through, and the district appreciated those efforts. But once again TurnKey had to break away from best business practices.

BUILDING WITHOUT FINISHED PLANS

Normally in construction, the contractor (TurnKey here) sends out the architect's plans to obtain bids from subcontractors. The contractor then selects the qualified subcontractor with the lowest bid and issues contracts for the work to be performed. This locks in the costs to the contractor, who can then manage the project with its profit and overhead predetermined. In this case, TurnKey was not able to put the insufficiently developed plans out for bids in advance.

Instead, all of TurnKey's design resources had to focus on fixing or completing the belowground infrastructure and then prioritizing what was imperative to complete next, creating a chaotic organizational bottleneck. In addition, because of the increased risks posed by less-than-complete plans, subcontractors submitted higher bids. The combination of these issues made the projects incredibly risky and unmanageable from the very beginning.

And because these projects represented such a large portion of TurnKey's business, the company could not effectively manage its own business. By not sticking to best practices, TurnKey was setting itself up for disaster.

Even so, in August 2004, TurnKey and the district opened the new schools, and by running on a traditional schedule the district saved millions in operating costs. The "impossible" was made a reality with a massive effort, great risks, and huge costs. The extent of those costs would only become clear later.

LESSONS LEARNED

- Do not vary from proper business practice or procedures to meet clients' needs.

- Retain excellent legal counsel. When things start to turn against the entrepreneur, have counsel focus on protecting the family and the company.

- Maintain proper errors & omissions (E&O) and directors & officers (D&O) insurance at all times, even when strapped for cash.

CHAPTER 3

A DECADE OF LEGAL WOES

Outrageous growth takes enormous amounts of cash. Both construction and development are capital intensive, and in early 2004 TurnKey invited investment bankers in to explore raising capital so that I was not the only source of money for the company. When companies work largely on bonded projects, are vertically integrated, and have their own manufacturing plant, capital becomes even more important.

Bonding is a form of insurance some clients require. If the construction company has a performance problem, the bonding insurance company will come in and complete the project. To qualify for a bond, a construction company has to have a significant amount of net worth and, importantly, the owners of the company have to guarantee personally any liability or losses. Because most TurnKey projects were bonded, our corporate balance sheet had to be substantial. In addition, I had to sign personal guarantees that, in case of claims and losses, my personal net worth would be available.

The investment bankers asked the TurnKey CFO to develop a refined cash flow report in March 2004. His document showed that TurnKey would have a tight cash flow in the fall, but that we'd make it through the year without the need for any new capital. In response, the investment bankers counseled TurnKey that if we could make it through the year without raising capital, the company's valuation would be far greater in 2005, and thus the cost of capital would be far less expensive. So we decided to wait a year.

However, by July 2004 TurnKey's financial data began to look odd. The numbers just didn't seem right. After a quick analysis we determined that the construction teams hadn't accurately updated the project cost reports that fed into the CFO's key database. The costs had been under-reported, and the result was that TurnKey's cash flow forecast from March had swung to the tune of $10 million. This resulted in an instant $5 million loss for the company. TurnKey was headed off the cliff.

PRIVATE EQUITY

TurnKey quickly hired an investment banking firm to raise $20 million. Within forty-five days it found five private equity firms that offered $20 million for a 20 percent equity stake, giving TurnKey a valuation of $100 million. It seemed disaster had been averted.

One Los Angeles–based private equity firm had a nice proposal, and several of the TurnKey founders had connections or relationships with the firm's principals, regarding them as great guys and excellent potential partners. The private equity firm wanted at least two months to perform its due diligence and fund the transaction.

Meanwhile, the investment banker TurnKey had hired was intrigued with a Vancouver-based firm that offered funding in thirty days, but this Canada enterprise wanted to be exclusive, meaning no other firm could perform due diligence at the same time. For the investment banker it would mean a new private equity partner for future transactions. We figured that quicker funding would be better for everyone, so we went with the Vancouver company that none of us knew.

It happened that Sam Belzberg, who allegedly became a billionaire in the 1980s as a corporate raider, owned the Vancouver firm. Perhaps the investment banker discounted stories of Belzberg's character or assumed the tiger had changed his stripes.

In any case, the private equity firm did its due diligence and in thirty days—on a Monday in October 2004—was set to fund the investment. On the Friday before funding, the leading manager for Belzberg pressured the TurnKey CFO to pay any outstanding payables with our remaining $1.5 million of cash. The reasoning was that since TurnKey was closing the investment on Monday, the company might as well get a head start paying bills. Despite his reservations, the CFO went ahead and paid off the payables with TurnKey's remaining money.

Over that weekend the same Belzberg manager asked for a cash report. On Monday, Belzberg called me and said, "Harry, we love your company and still want to do the deal. However, over the weekend we received a cash report that shows you have no more cash. So it looks right now like you need us more than we need you. We'll still make the investment, but we want 80 percent of the equity rather than 20 percent."

My jaw dropped. I thanked him for the call but politely said we would pursue other options. I immediately phoned the investment banker and asked him to telephone the Los Angeles–based firm we knew.

THE WHEELS ARE WOBBLING

Private equity companies are not venture capital firms. They only make investments in more mature and stable entities. TurnKey had attracted the interest of private equity firms because its scale and growth were huge, and we were doing everything with an eye to being world class. However, TurnKey had just five years of operations, and we were in a relatively risky marketplace.

The private equity firm we knew in California commenced due diligence, but within a week the principal told me that an investment probably wouldn't work. Three months had passed since our initial contact, and TurnKey had blown out its cash, weakening the company substantially.

My heart sank, and I have to say I was totally overwhelmed. Rarely in my life had I felt so backed into a corner without the ability to figure out a solution. And although I always surrounded myself with smart, well-qualified people, none of my team knew what to do either. At the end of the day, it was mostly my butt on the line.

The stress was enormous: TurnKey entered into forced bankruptcy, and we had to lay off fantastic employees, abandon projects, give up new contracts worth tens of millions, and watch all that we had built dissolve before our eyes. What had been worth $100 million only five months earlier was now not worth a penny. Even worse, I had personal guarantees on a multitude of bank loans, leases, and bonding.

BANKRUPTCY

Although my wife, Linda, and I had an elaborate personal estate plan, our focus had been on taxes and our plans to transfer the wealth from us to our children. I recall precisely when the financial advisor had asked us if we wanted creditor protection. He asked us twice, and twice we replied, "No, we have always paid our bills, banks have always loved us, and we live conservatively." So our complex and elaborate estate plan had absolutely no provisions to protect our wealth from lawsuits or creditors.

Linda and I had personally guaranteed approximately $5.6 million in loans from Bank of America and had unlimited exposure to The Hartford, TurnKey's bonding company.

If I knew then what I know now, I would have hired a consultant to work through the mess and negotiate settlements one at a time. My wife and I had $25 million worth of personal assets that we should have methodically sold and used to pay off debts. If we had proceeded with a sound financial plan, we probably would have had $10 million or more in assets left.

Instead, I was referred to a well-reputed (and insanely expensive) bankruptcy attorney, who held preliminary discussions with Bank of America and The Hartford. After a couple of weeks of negotiations, he recommended that we file personal Chapter 11.

Now personal Chapter 11 filings are rare. Most people don't have $25 million in assets, as we did. More common personal bankruptcy filings are Chapter 7 liquidations, which allow the parties to nearly walk away from the process after a few months and at nominal costs.

Furthermore, the more assets there are in an estate, the more any fight turns into a feeding frenzy for attorneys. Our personal bankruptcy attorney billed $1.5 million in eighteen months, and countless other attorneys also fed on our estate. We suddenly understood why lawyers are often called sharks.

After twelve months of living under continual stress from the bankruptcy, Linda left me. Our twenty-year marriage was over. Shortly thereafter, one of our daughters attempted suicide because of the stress related to our divorce. Fortunately, she survived the ordeal and is thriving today.

MISTAKEN LIQUIDATION

Eighteen months after we filed for bankruptcy, Linda sent a letter to our attorney asking him to convert the bankruptcy from a Chapter 11 to a Chapter 7. She was starting a new job that day and didn't want to worry about the onerous financial proceedings any more. Several hours later, she tried to recant, thinking that perhaps she made a mistake. It was too late. The conversion had begun already.

Moreover, when Linda directed our attorney to do something against my wishes, she created a conflict between his two clients (Linda and me), and the attorney had to resign. The case converted instantly—and unilaterally—from a reorganization to a liquidation, which meant that we were about to lose control of the process. Not only were we left without an attorney, but we would also have to turn over the remaining assets—by that point about $20 million—to a trustee.

Ironically, the Santa Barbara school district remained by far the most aggressive creditor of our personal bankruptcy estate. Though their claims were completely unsupported—the district was a creditor of

TurnKey but not of our personal estate—the district's lawyers kept fighting every step of the way. They were so aggressive that attorneys for Bank of America and The Hartford sat back and let the district bear the legal fees related to the fighting. Because of the burden the fees were placing on the estate, the trustee finally gave the district a token settlement to get them to back away.

That was not the end. To up the ante, the school district's lawyer shopped their case to several district attorneys, hoping to initiate criminal proceedings against me. Initially the court rejected these claims because this was a case of a company growing too fast and going out of business—nothing criminal about it. However, the California Attorney General's office ultimately convened grand jury proceedings.

THE GRAND JURY

The grand jury proceedings lasted three weeks, and forty-four people testified. We never received a notice of these hearings, and I had no idea they were even going on. I had no representation, no chance to question witnesses' testimony. It was a unilateral sham.

In the end, the attorneys for the state recommended prosecution for thirteen subcontractors' invoices paid outside of the ten-day statutory limit, a little understood statute under California law. The fact that TurnKey had paid many of these invoices within about two weeks of receiving its own payment counted for nothing. The law required payment within ten days.

The state took those thirteen late invoices and converted them into seventy-four counts against three other people and me. These proceedings probably cost the state government $2 million, beyond an estimated $4 million paid to the school district's attorney.

IT'S ILLEGAL TO GO BANKRUPT

About four years into this case, my attorneys and I finally started figuring out what it was all about. Essentially, in California, if a contractor is paid and doesn't pay its subcontractors within ten days, that is a potential felony known as diversion of funds. No proof of intent or knowledge by the contractor is required.

Here's how it works: Your company goes bankrupt, your subcontractors aren't paid, and your personal guarantees for bonding and the credit line causes a personal bankruptcy. You lose all of your personal assets. Now you're also automatically guilty of a non-intent diversion of funds and liable for criminal charges. Only in California!

By using a grand jury rather than state or county courts, the prosecution avoided a preliminary hearing in which we would have had an opportunity to receive representation and conduct cross-examination. Instead, the case lingered for a decade.

In the end, it never went to trial. In December 2014 the judge mediated the case, eliminating the felony charges and finding that there was no moral wrongdoing or criminal intent.

So, after ten years, the entire ordeal was over and behind me. What an incredible waste of government resources and personal worry about potential felony convictions.

Because of my personal guarantees to the bank and bonding companies, my wife and I lost our entire estate of $25 million, our marriage ended, and we nearly lost one of our daughters. In addition, the ripple effect reached my parents, other family members, and several friends.

For ten years my career was largely limited to various consulting engagements. I had to wait until all the pending issues were resolved before taking on any serious CEO roles or attempting to start up a company again. I felt like an airplane that had been in a holding pattern for a decade.

However, I'm happy to report I've come in for a smooth landing. At a trade show in Atlanta in January 2012, I met the woman of my dreams, and Heather and I have been together ever since. I moved to Arizona to be with her and her two teenage sons, and with my four daughters, we're a bit like the Brady Bunch.

Heather and I were married in June 2014. She is my life partner, and every day is filled with happiness and love.

LESSONS LEARNED

- Typically, entrepreneurs are trained to take on huge stress. When things go bad, however, the trauma to families and friends can be immense. Entrepreneurs must protect their families.

- As an ongoing practice, businesses should always retain cash balances or have significant cash reserves.

- Asset protection should be as important as life insurance. Set aside a significant start-over fund as a minimum.

- The purpose of creditor protection is to protect the family, and it should be an important part of any estate plan. Don't be arrogant or naïve.

- Use bankruptcy attorneys to help educate those in the business, and learn how to leverage the threat of bankruptcy to the creditors.

- Consider hiring a specialty financial advisor (CPA, lawyer, or other expert) to help negotiate through all issues before filing bankruptcy. Owning and running a business can be overwhelming, and entrepreneurs need outside resources to help them.

- Bankruptcy attorneys cannot give advice on asset protection. They work for the future bankrupt estate, and it is a conflict for them to give advice on self-protection.

- Bankruptcy attorneys aren't effective at keeping entrepreneurs out of bankruptcy. That's where their money is made.

- Use an asset protection specialist, even up until the end. Think of it as insurance.

PART TWO

BUSINESS MODELS & CHALLENGES

CHAPTER 4

BUSINESS MODELS

*"You know all of our people have to eat every week,
regardless of the economy, right?"*

Several entrepreneurs who volunteered to be part of this project had a variety of fundamental challenges to their business models. In these chapters they discuss diversifying your business, using outside capital, recurring revenues, and the particular challenges of family businesses.

DIVERSIFY, DIVERSIFY, DIVERSIFY

Most of us have heard about the importance of diversifying investments. Entrepreneurs, however, typically lack investment diversity because their business often represents a disproportionately high percentage of their estate value. Further, an entrepreneur's company equity is typically illiquid, which only underscores the vital importance of diversifying as early and often as possible to help offset risks. When the big payday occurs and the company is sold, the entrepreneur needs discipline and dedication to diversify his estate.

"When one is being acquired by another company, often the deal structure has a significant percentage of stock associated with it," explains

Alejandro Rivas Micoud, a Spanish telecom and technology entrepreneur who made and lost a couple of fortunes. "Anybody who goes into that deal should not have done so—no matter how much [the buyers] explain what sort of fantastic company they are and that they are the best thing since toast. As soon as they can, entrepreneurs should sell the stock and diversify. I'd recommend they put everything in an index fund or something like that and not play with it."

Alejandro, whom we'll read about in more detail later, got a second shot at a fortune after his company was acquired in an all-stock deal. He watched the stock value go from its privately held, pre-IPO value, through the IPO, more than double in value, then be worth nearly nothing at all.

Throughout this book, you'll read examples of the consequences of not having a diverse portfolio. Andrew Dumke went from having about $100 million to eating rice and beans from emergency supplies in his basement.

Andrew had been a sharp serial entrepreneur who invested well in companies for decades. His family had created enormous wealth from an earlier sale of a business to General Electric. He received a significant portfolio of GE stock but didn't diversify that investment.

"When people talk about investing in the stock market, they always say diversify a bit; don't keep all your eggs in one basket," Andrew explained. "You don't want to overdiversify, but don't have just one stock. That's important advice. If I hadn't had 100 percent of my net worth in GE during the financial crisis, when GE stock went down 90 percent, it wouldn't have been so economically devastating for me. So having a few more stocks is a good thing. Now I have a more diverse basket of stocks. I could take more market hits before I would have that devastating effect."

When I sold MuniFinancial in 1997, I had diversified our investments quite a bit with the proceeds from the sale of the company. However, my longtime financial advisor told me to stop trying to optimize the return of the portfolio.

He told me, "Harry, for all these years you were investing to maximize the return on your investment. Now you have a large enough portfolio that you need to be more concerned about preservation with a nice steady return." That was an important turning point. If my advisor hadn't called me on it, I'm not sure I would have changed my behavior.

START-UP ADVICE: OTHER PEOPLE'S MONEY

The other lesson Alejandro and I both learned is to be careful starting up your next new venture after a huge payout. Studies have shown that even though an entrepreneur has been successful with a first company, it's less likely that the second company will follow suit.

Arrogance can get in the way of wanting to use other people's money. You might be tempted to think, "Why should I have investors? I have $10 million in the bank! I made it myself the first time." Don't go there! Like me, Alejandro learned this lesson the hard way. He started a company and ended up losing €4 to €5 million at a time when he lost everything else in the tech crash. His current thought is, "I would never again want to get into a start-up on my own. In addition, I think that having people looking over your shoulder, seeing your blind spots— whether at the board level, your management team level, the investor level, or hopefully all three—is hugely important in any start-up."

That's great advice. Being accountable to other investors really does increase the performance of entrepreneurs.

RECURRING VERSUS ONETIME BUSINESS

A common theme that I heard from entrepreneurs is the vulnerability and volatility of project-based revenue as the basis for the company. During good times, companies that rely on these kinds of funds can be wildly profitable and fast growing, but when the tide changes, things can unwind quickly.

My first company, MuniFinancial, had 1,500 thirty-year contracts to administer some aspect of our clients' municipal bond issues. Most of these contracts were paid quarterly in advance and had automatic consumer price index (CPI) adjustments built into them. The business was perfectly predictable and impervious to economic cycles. It was a relatively easy business to manage, grow, and operate.

Comparing MuniFinancial to TurnKey was like looking at day and night. TurnKey was all project based, with an average contract size of about $10 million. Each contract would last twelve to eighteen months and was subject to government funding approval. The volatility made managing the company incredibly difficult and risky and ultimately ended in bankruptcy.

IMPORTANCE OF REVENUE MODELS

During my interviews, several entrepreneurs stressed the importance of the revenue model. Take, for example, Bob Verdun's software company, which he grew through the 1990s at a consistent 35 percent compounded growth rate.

Bob Verdun earned a BS from Eastern Michigan University in industrial technology and is CEO of the Detroit-area software company Computer Facility Integrators. He successfully transitioned the company from project-based revenue to recurring revenue after getting hit hard several times. He currently has more than $26 million in sales and about 130 employees. YPO member.

Times were very good for Bob and his company. By 1999 his Detroit-area firm had sales of $15 million and 150 employees. His customers included Ford, General Motors, and most of the leading technology companies—Motorola, Palm, 3com, Lucent, AT&T, Intel, Ameritech, and SBC. By the fall of that year, he had cash offers of $25 million to buy his firm.

Within sixty days, however, his company was almost worthless, because of the impact of the tech crash of 1999–2000.

Bob said, "Literally, in December 1999, the phone started to ring, and it wasn't an automatic, 'Hey, we're canceling your project.' For example, 3com called, and the worst part of it was that they said, 'Well, we've got some budget issues. We're still going forward, but we can't start it for another sixty days, so we're going to push it to the next year's budget.'

"Some of the projects were canceled, but many of our big customers would just stall, or defer, or not tell us anything. That really amplified the impact in terms of our first round of cuts not being deep enough. We crashed hard—an instant drop of 60 percent in revenue—in December 1999."

In 2000, Bob's company's revenue plummeted further, from $15 million to less than $4 million. He stated, "Through the Christmas break of '99, I was trying to figure out how to save the company, determine the people I could keep, and whatever avenues I could count on."

Among his biggest liabilities were leases for offices throughout the United States. Bob went on to say, "We ended up doing a prepackaged bankruptcy, which, you know, General Motors did back then, and it was a pretty big deal. We went through the entire process in under ninety days. Now there are other companies who've done it, but back then it was unheard of. But it was to save the company, because I didn't have enough cash to last longer. I had to drive it through the process quickly."

THINK STRATEGICALLY

After surviving those dark days, which lasted roughly through 2001, Bob re-examined his company and developed two core principles for the future of the business: a diversified revenue base and recurring revenues.

He said, "I guess one of the lessons learned during that period is that I was adamant this is never happening to me again. I started looking at the big picture. How do we create a business we want to have versus reacting to the marketplace and just going along where the world takes you? We really focused much more on strategy and building the business going forward. Therefore we changed our projects to recurring revenue, and we took strategic planning seriously from that point forward.

"Fast forward to the Great Recession in 2008: We had 75 percent recurring revenue completely diversified by every segment and industry you could think of. So in 2008, we were at about $14 million in sales. From a revenue perspective, we pretty much got back to where we were before."

However, by this time Bob had built a much more stable business with only about ninety employees. In fact, in 2008, the revenues of his business still grew about 2 percent, even though some of his customers were hit hard. In 2013 Bob's business did about $26 million in sales, had grown to about 130 employees, and was highly profitable.

Summarizing the benefits of thinking strategically, Bob said, "You get more time to react to fix the problem, which is why in 2008 we were fine, and we got through without a hiccup. We did miss our earnings target because of our revenue drop, but we were fine; we didn't lose any money.

"I think it starts with strategy," he added. "You have to build a business that's sustainable and structurally sound. It has to have the right kind of components to make it safe. You know all of our people have to eat every week regardless of the economy, right?"

I believe the way Bob converted his company should be an inspiration for all entrepreneurs saddled with the stress of running a onetime-revenue model of business. Think strategically, and try to develop a way for your contracts to recur. It will change everything for the better.

A FAMILY BUSINESS

Jim Glazer is a bright, hardworking guy. He graduated near the top of his class at Duke and later completed an MBA at the University of Michigan. He then worked at Arthur Young and Price Waterhouse in their Entrepreneurial Services Groups. He knew he eventually wanted to run and grow a business of his own.

Jim Glazer is a Duke undergraduate and has a University of Michigan MBA and CPA. He led Elliott Manufacturing, a family business that developed specialty trucks. Located in Omaha, Nebraska, the firm had as much as $65 million in sales. YPO member.

Jim ended up joining a specialty-truck-manufacturing business that his father had acquired. Jim, his brother, and his father grew the company, which was located in Omaha, Nebraska, from about $2.5 million in sales in 1993 to some $25 million in 2000. Personally he was doing well, dropping about $1 million onto his tax return each year. By 2002 he had become president of the company.

Over the next several years, the company expanded and diversified, but its profits continued to shrink. By 2007, the firm was generating $65 million in sales but with less profit than there had been with $25 million in sales.

"In hindsight, I realize how disengaged I was from the business," Jim said candidly, "especially in the early 2000s. In fact, none of us were engaged. My dad was out in Arizona. I didn't feel very involved, because my dad still wanted to keep his fingers in things, and my brother obviously wasn't engaged. Business suffered, and I personally suffered. At the end of the day, I just didn't feel good about myself, even though I had all this money.

"In 2011, we hit the low point," Jim said, "because we were still trying to turn things around. We were breaking even in cash flow, but we missed our projection. First, our CFO quit, and shortly thereafter, our controller quit. Right after that our payroll person tried to submit two payrolls at the same time accidentally. So the bank got skittish. It took all our money out of our personal accounts. Afterward the bank wouldn't talk with us for a week—and that was over the Thanksgiving holiday!"

The story of the Glazer family business continues in later chapters.

LESSONS LEARNED

- When you have liquidity from selling all or a portion of your business, make sure you diversify the assets.

- Do not hold onto a large portfolio of the stock you've acquired after the sale of your company. Liquidate it as soon as possible into a diversified portfolio with only moderate risk.

- When starting up a new company after the successful sale of your previous business, make sure to have outside investors. You'll perform better and have less risk of losing wealth.

- Don't be overconfident when starting a second company. Studies show that even entrepreneurs who were successful with a first enterprise are likely to fail with a second.

- Onetime project-based business models are highly volatile and therefore risky for the entrepreneur. If possible, convert the business from a project-based model to a recurring-revenue model.

- Diversify the composition of your clients in every way possible: geography, segments, percentage of your sales, and so on.

- Deal with leadership and family transition issues openly. The consequences of ignoring them can be catastrophic.

CHAPTER 5

A UNICORN STORY

*"When we bought our competitor,
we lost our ability to validate our technology.
There was no other company to point to."*

Andrew Dumke is a hard-charging serial entrepreneur who has made and lost huge fortunes and made them back again. He was a board member and investor of DataWorks, a "unicorn" company that skyrocketed from a $10 million valuation to being worth more than $2 billion. He then acquired two companies with mixed results.

Andrew Dumke, a true entrepreneur, dropped out of the University of Utah in the 1980s because he wanted to start a software business. Using family money, he invested in numerous companies, including one that grew to a market cap of $2 billion—DataWorks/Epicor. YPO member.

"In YPO," Andrew said, "we distinguish between those who came into the family business and those who were hired guns or entrepreneurs. I've had a little bit of all three. My father and grandfather were quite successful early on, and so I was fairly wealthy from the sale of a family business. I was more interested in the entrepreneurial world when I was in college, which I found ridiculously boring. I was studying computer science.

"So I dropped out of the University of Utah in the early '80s to start some kind of a software company. It was the days of Apple II computers; the IBM PC hadn't yet been announced, and so it was a real growth industry. I sensed that, and I moved to San Francisco. I had enough money to be able to invest in certain things and to support myself, so I didn't have to flip burgers to eat."

STERLING PACIFIC

Andrew continued, "I showed up in San Francisco when I was twenty-two and found some people who were writing a software program to do business graphics for the Apple II. They claimed with some credibility that the graphics of that time were just hideous. I convinced them that my friend and I could market that software, so we formed the first company, Sterling Pacific.

"We picked up some accounts, and over time the company morphed into a very early version of what we would now call desktop publishing. We could take text data and turn it into graphs; we could take the graphs and insert them into flow text. It was more sophisticated than a lot of other things that were in the competitive market space.

"But the software was being marketed by a couple of twenty-two-year-olds who didn't even look twenty-two. We did the best we could. We learned on the job, since there were no books to read. I probably put $10,000 of personal money into the venture, which helped it to get off the ground. We got an office space. We got packaging and graphics. We could do some business trips. It wasn't a huge amount of money, but we didn't have to hit penniless creativity. The big setback was that my partner got lung cancer in his mid-twenties and soon died.

"At the end of the day this business didn't make much money, but it got our name out there to other business connections. Nobody had ever described to me the value of networking. I didn't realize it. At a certain point I just handed the company to its distributors and turned over the software to them."

PACIFIC MEZZANINE FUND

After a stint with a financial software firm, Andrew started doing project work for a private equity group.

He remembered, "After my first project, the principals thought I seemed like a smart kid and maybe I could help them with their deals. It was 1987, during the leveraged buyout boom.

"I got to know their business and really wanted to be involved. It seemed like a hell of a lot less work than software: It's scalable, and you could get a lot of other people to do the work for you. I joined the group, and my first project was for no pay.

"We did our first deal together, which gave me the opportunity to receive some interest and invest a bit of money in a company that made recirculating pumps. The company had a high market share of the pumps for birdbaths and waterfalls in California, and we bought it.

"We realized that we liked working together. The group saw I added value to them, and I realized they definitely added value to what I was trying to do. After a year we sold the pump company and got our money out. It was not a gain and not a loss, but it was a valuable experience. We then looked at several other companies in the aircraft and modular-homes industries."

DATAWORKS/EPICOR

Andrew continued his story: "The next deal we did around 1992 turned out to be a huge hit: a software company in the enterprise resource planning (ERP) market. It was a small company with about fifteen employees doing about $10 million in revenue and needed some expansion capital. My expertise in software was very helpful this time, and their expertise in finance was also very helpful. It happened to be a great hit, a confluence of tides.

"I believed in this company. I took some family money and stuck it into the deal. We ended up being the first outside investors, which ultimately ended up being one of the largest ERP vendors in the world. DataWorks did a bunch of acquisitions, and it ultimately became a public company called Epicor. My initial investment grew to be worth about $40 million at its peak.

"The ERP market in the 1990s was a three-year preview of what would happen in the Internet market after 2000. These ERP companies came out of nowhere and boomed into being public companies worth way more money than they should have been. Some of the companies are very successful today, such as Oracle and SAP. They are survivors of that era. Most melted down to obscurity or were merged into other companies.

"A lot of the companies grew to have unsustainable valuations," Andrew pointed out. "When we invested in DataWorks, it had a $10 million valuation; later at its peak it was worth about $2 billion. I was the second largest personal shareholder, just after the founder.

"I had a seat on the board, and we debated about how we were going to grow. I heard internal projections from management, but I wasn't able to parse out a decision made on facts from one made on partial facts or a decision made strictly on emotion. I needed an honest assessment of what the next few quarters were going to look like.

"I was not very experienced, however; I had zero experience at the board level of a public company. I was just a kid from Idaho who hadn't finished college. The first company I'd founded had three people; now I was at the senior level of a public company with 1,500 people worldwide."

INSTITUTIONAL SELF-DELUSION

"I had a large stake and really wanted to believe my little $40 million piece was going to be worth $100 million, maybe even more," Andrew said. "You look at some of the comps—Larry Ellison at Oracle, back then he was worth $5 billion. Well, we thought DataWorks could keep going. Our software was better than Oracle's; there was a process of institutional self-delusion.

"Several things happened: One, we were really smart, but it turns out we hadn't given enough credit to luck. We did pretty well with the cards we were dealt, but it was still a card game. Somebody else could get better cards than you.

"During the mid-'90s, the ERP market was like selling sex. The companies would come to us, and customers would have to make appointments months in advance to get a sales presentation. We would play hard to get on purpose. It really had a way of completely warping the decision-making process.

"More and more evidence came in that this just wasn't working right. At first, we missed internal projections, but we were able to meet expectations for a couple of quarters.

"We'd been working on a really big deal for eighteen months or so, but it was won by one of our competitors. It was so shocking to lose that deal that the board decided that we needed to buy our competitor and become the big gorilla in this market."

AN UNSTRATEGIC ACQUISITION

Andrew explained, "We bought that company and paid way too much, and that was death knell for the company. All the other ERP companies were scaling down. With Y2K coming up, everybody had to replace their software, but the sales push was ending, because the available customers had already made their decisions.

"DataWorks went from $35 per share and started falling. Inside the board we told ourselves, 'Well, we're smart people. We'll know how to solve this. We'll be the only one selling this particular ERP technology.' But we didn't think about the ramifications to the prospective customers.

"The DataWorks software was based on a certain underlying technology that was different than the mainstream market. When we had our competitor, we could always point at them and say, 'Well, it's not that different, you know. That company over there is using it.' But when we bought our competitor, we lost our ability to validate the technology. There was no other company to point to."

THE GREAT FALL

"First, we shot ourselves in the foot by buying our competitor and paying too much just as the market fell out from under us," Andrew said. "We were too arrogant to figure out that our decision-making process was just screwed up, so the stock had a slow, miserable decline. Then the company ran out of money and did a secondary rights offering. Still believing how great it was, I put $8 million back in at $10 per share; in early 2000, the stock hit a low of $0.65 per share.

"I had invested lots of time and a big chunk of my family fortune. Then as the stock went down, my wife told me to sell it, and of course, I wouldn't. That became a big thorn in our relationship.

"Two things happened that significantly softened that blow. First, because of the earlier success in DataWorks, I was made a partner of a private equity firm, so I had income. While I wasn't really living the life that I could have had with that nest egg, it didn't seem like such a tragedy. The second thing was the sale of my family's business to General Electric, which boomed like crazy in the 1990s. What had been a nice family fortune became a huge family fortune.

"After the time at Pacific Mezzanine and DataWorks, I decided to raise capital and buy a division from Epicor that sold software in the aerospace and defense markets that managed maintenance, repair, and overhaul. The new company was called Avexus, and I became the CEO.

"I took the job on September 6, 2001," Andrew remembered. "Our target customers were airlines and suppliers to airlines. Five days later, the terror attacks involving four airlines significantly impacted the industry. It was another bad hand of cards. After running Avexus for several years, I had strategic disagreements with the board, and I was fired.

"After Avexus, I spent a couple of years stewing. Since GE was paying a dividend, I had enough money to live comfortably, but I didn't feel quite ready to retire. I was only in my mid-forties. I was a member of YPO, which was incredibly valuable, because I could see what other people were doing. I was learning volumes in comparison to just having my own limited experience.

"I decided that I wanted to have a business with one of the guys I had worked with at my last firm. Back then I had tried to promote him to vice president, but the board squashed the promotion. He'd had an accident when he was a kid, lost his voice, and now spoke with a *Godfather*-like rasp. He was a handsome guy, very smart, very strategic, and a good sales guy. He was responsible for most of our successful sales.

"Here was a guy that most people wouldn't hire just because of a somewhat unattractive physical characteristic, but I knew he was smart, and I had a little bit of cash. I decided to buy several Popsicle stand-size businesses and put him in charge of them."

TIMELY MEDICAL INNOVATIONS

Andrew continued, "We ran across a business that had a large market share worldwide, making something you probably don't think about much: infection-control goggles. If you get your teeth cleaned or have surgery, the medical staff wears them for protection and to not expose anyone to potentially infectious fluids. At first doctors and technicians were ill prepared to meet federal standards. They used welding goggles!

"This company—Timely Medical Innovations—designed a sleek, disposable, low-cost version of these goggles that met federal standards and was manufactured here in San Diego. They cost about three cents to manufacture and were sold on average for eighty cents, so there was a great margin. The company had grown from a startup to about $3 million in revenue with about $2 million in earnings before taxes, depreciation, and amortization (EBIDTA).

"The owners weren't getting along, so they were trying to sell, but it was an odd deal: They were essentially trying to sell the company as a product with no employees to operate it, almost just a concept. You buy it and have to add people yourself. Well, that was perfect, because I had the guy I was trying to find a job for. We bought the company for a very attractive price and 100 percent leverage. We had literally no capital in it at all, and with $2 million in EBIDTA, what could be the downside?

"Almost immediately there were influenza scares around the world, and the sales of this little company went from $3 million in revenue up to $10 million in revenue, and an EBIDTA of about $6 million."

DIVORCE AND RECESSION

"Meanwhile, my two years of depression after the Avexus debacle caused my marriage to fail," said Andrew. "That was at the beginning of '08, just before the financial panic, when one of the biggest companies hit during the Great Recession was GE.

"At the beginning of that year I had nearly $40 million of GE stock. I also had this little company, Timely, that was highly leveraged. I owned 90 percent of it, but I would have had to pay off all the debt in order to access the cash.

"And then my wife wanted a divorce. Divorce law in California is pretty severe. She hired a fairly aggressive attorney and got financial people who looked at my personal balance sheet and the profit of the company. The court said, 'You're making $6 million a year from the company as well as another million from GE dividends, so you owe her as much as $3 million a year.'

"The financial market was starting to melt down, but I was so distracted by the divorce that I wasn't really paying attention to what was going on in the world.

"My wife's attorney reached out to my attorney, and we struck a deal for me to buy her out of our community property. I borrowed money in a margin account against my GE stock to pay her $5 million, plus support of more than $1 million a year. I also had $11 million of debt at Timely, and by legal agreement, I had to refinance our house so that the mortgage was no longer in her name."

GE STOCK AND THE MARGIN ACCOUNT

Andrew said, "I went from an incredibly liquid balance sheet of $40 million in liquid assets and no debt to having $6 million of debt and a company that was cash-flow rich but highly leveraged. Then in November '08, when Lehman Brothers went bankrupt, you couldn't refinance a mortgage, you couldn't borrow money, you couldn't refinance small business debt. GE stock plummeted from $40 to $5 a share, and they cut off access to my margin account.

"When GE cut its dividend to nothing, Timely wasn't paying me a salary. My income went to zero. My ability to tap liquidity went to zero. I was under court order to refinance the house, but couldn't. I had mounting legal bills. I had payments on my mortgage that were overdue and rapidly fell into default. When I told my ex's attorney I was going to default on the support payments because I couldn't pay them, he thought I was joking. I had been worth more than $40 million just two months earlier.

"By December '08 I couldn't even take money out of an ATM. Luckily, I had been raised in Mormon country, and, like many Mormons, I had food, money, and emergency supplies in my basement. I started eating that food and using that money—about $50,000 in cash in the safe."

Andrew explained the reasoning behind his emergency supplies: "I have fire insurance, I have auto insurance, I have medical insurance. I've got all these insurance policies that they tell you to have, and that I hardly ever use. But I lived in Florida through two major hurricanes, I lived in San Francisco through a major earthquake, and I lived in both Idaho and San Diego through major wildfires, and disasters seem a bigger risk to me.

"To me, filling your basement with six months of food, which costs $10,000, is cheap insurance. Adding some cash and some tradable things such as gold also seems like really cheap insurance. And that $50,000 in cash saved my life, as well as my ego.

"I guess I could have gone to all my friends and said, 'Hey, brother, can you spare five grand?' But I didn't have to do that. I didn't have to go on public assistance, though I was really close. I was eating beans and rice, while trying to keep my kids from finding out how bad it had gotten.

"I also started selling things on eBay, beginning with my own and my friends' music CDs. I'd sell three CDs for $15, and my friends told me to just keep the money. You know, it saved my life. I was generating about $20,000 a month selling extra stuff out of my house.

"My car was breaking down, but I couldn't get it fixed, and I was stuck with a private jet that I couldn't give away, let alone sell. You have to appreciate how rapidly things spin out of control. When you can't put gas in your car, when your credit cards don't work, when your credit rating is plummeting, when you have to think about each and every purchase at the grocery store, and you can't buy a pair of shoes for your kids—all of a sudden, the mechanics of day-to-day living sap your energy.

"Meanwhile, Timely was doing great. Though it continued to grow, I still couldn't touch the money. I just kept trying to recapitalize and rebuild as I ground through a really ugly divorce. Since I paid my ex millions, she had all the cash, and I held all the debt.

"Just after we signed the divorce papers in '09, I received a completely out-of-the-blue, unsolicited call to buy Timely for about $20 million net to me. After going through that near-death experience financially, even though I could have optimized the deal and probably gotten more, I took it. That was $20 million cash in my pocket to pay off all my debts. At the end of the day I still had $15 million. Meanwhile, the GE stock climbed back up in value.

"I bought another company making LED lights, and it's now a lot bigger than Timely. We're about $15 million in revenue and about $3 million in EBIDTA, but without all the debt. So now I'm back. And let me tell you, I don't go to any nostalgic parties for the year 2008!"

ANDREW'S TAKEAWAYS

"One thing I learned," said Andrew, "is that debt cuts both ways. Always maintain liquidity. If I hadn't had that money in my basement safe, that 'rainy-day cash,' I would have been living on assistance or borrowing money from friends.

"Second, I've learned to keep things really, really simple. Simple businesses are easier than hard businesses. At DataWorks, we had a complex sales cycle, we had the development cycle, we had all these things with a thin balance sheet and huge overhead. As soon as things turned, they turned rapidly. We went from being a $2 billion market-cap company to a $20 million cap company in no time, from a company with a couple hundred million dollars in the bank to no money in the bank. When you're going in the wrong direction, liquidity can disappear fast. I bet the people at Lehman Brothers might say the same thing.

"Number three, hang with the right people. The wrong people can screw you if they have the opportunity. Business is hard enough without people shooting at you.

"Number four, definitely maintain your personal physical and mental health. I let myself become depressed at home, which cost me my marriage. Looking back, that wasn't necessarily a bad thing, and I'm really happy now. But if my goal had been to stay married to my first wife, I needed to keep my mental and emotional faculties up.

"All the really big downfalls I've had somehow involved lawyers and a feeling that they're 'going to fight until everything is gone.' Even over a few dollars here or there. That's the law of the jungle. With tens of millions or hundreds of millions, people fight vigorously. And sometimes stupidly. The end result is not always justice."

GETTING ADVICE, NOT HELP

"My YPO forum was very helpful," Andrew remembered. "I had tears streaming down my face as I explained my financial situation. I started with these baseline rules: 'I don't want any of your money. Don't offer me money. I want your ideas and I want them untainted by the notion that it might cost you money. Let's just take that off the table. I'm not looking for your money. I'm looking for your ideas on how to turn this around.'

"And I was proud of myself for my ability to regain my own humility really, really quickly. I quickly shifted into survivor mode. I wasn't angry, I wasn't resentful, I was just . . . this is what it is. And I think I made pretty good decisions. I was amazed how quickly I set up an online store and supported myself and my family for six or nine months.

"I remember feeling that I could either be overwhelmed by negative emotions or just choose to find it funny. I chose to laugh.

"My lowest moment was when I realized that my parents are very wealthy and when they die I'd be okay again. It felt horrible to think that my backup plan depended on my inheritance. But that's all I had to remind myself that it was not going to be like this for the rest of my life, that I was not going to die in poverty."

Andrew concluded, "When my grandfather was dying, he would say, 'Well, I can either suffer or just find it funny: I can't see, I can't hold my pee, and I can't hold my bowel.' He was one of the happiest men ever, and we all remember him. I think that attitude makes a massive difference in how you experience things and in the outcomes. Whether people want to see you succeed or not depends on how you carry yourself.

"I was injured badly in the woods once. I remember going into shock, and, when that happens, your chances of dying go up tenfold. What I've been describing is financial shock. Once you get there, your chances of surviving and getting back up to where you're financially okay are really slim. You have to start dealing with shit, like foreclosure on the house and switching the kids' schools, but a good attitude helps."

LESSONS LEARNED

- Be careful to manage debt, especially when loans are readily available.

- Always maintain liquidity. In a crisis $100,000 is worth more than $1 million when times are great.

- Keep cash in a safe or elsewhere as a rainy-day fund. In a crisis, that cash could be a godsend. Consider storing gold or other negotiable assets.

- Keep your business model simple. If it's too complex, it probably needs further development.

- Surround yourself with people of like mind, heart, and intent.

- Maintain your mental, emotional, and physical self, even through the worst of times.

- The more money you have, the more extreme the legal battles become. The attorneys will want to fight until all the money is gone.

CHAPTER 6

DOING BUSINESS WITH GOVERNMENT

"Government entities can be
arbitrary and capricious."

Of the thirty entrepreneurs interviewed, several had businesses with some level of governmental involvement. Doing business with government can be relatively stable, profitable, and predictable; it sometimes provides a sense of helping the betterment of society. On the other hand, government entities do not act like businesses when something goes wrong. They can be, and often are, arbitrary and capricious. They may be less concerned with budget or legal costs than for-profit ventures, so they may be vindictive despite legal or administrative expenses.

My experience with the school district in California as the CEO of TurnKey was an example of that. For a decade, that group plagued me, affecting me personally and professionally. The important thing to remember is that even with legal action public officials still collect their paychecks each and every week. Seeking revenge costs them nothing.

While being marginally innovative when dealing with governmental agencies may prove profitable, if you step too far outside the box, watch out! Companies such as 23andMe, Uber, and others may have compelling and game-changing businesses (and services to the market), but they will likely continue to be threatened by the various government bodies in their respective fields. I hope they maintain enormous D&O insurance policies and raise capital to pay their teams of lawyers.

THE SCOOTER STORE

To illustrate the difficulties of working with government, I interviewed Doug Harrison. He and his wife founded The SCOOTER Store and grew it into the largest retailer of electric scooters in the United States, with more than 3,000 employees and $500 million in revenue. Here's Doug's incredible story.

> Doug Harrison is a petroleum engineer with a degree from the Colorado School of Mines. Along with his wife, Susanna, he founded The SCOOTER Store and grew it into the largest seller of scooters and power wheelchairs in the world. Headquartered in Texas, the firm at one time had as much as $500 million in sales and more than 3,000 employees. YPO member.

"In 1991, my wife and I decided to start a business that we could do together," Doug said, "I was a petroleum engineer, and she was teaching computer software, and once we decided to take the plunge, the business took off quickly.

"In less than six weeks, we quit our jobs, sold our house in New Orleans, moved our home to Texas, launched the new business, and found out we were going to have our first baby! And that was only the beginning of the roller-coaster ride. Over the first seven years we grew from one store to five, but the more we grew, the more we lost money. Once we finally had the business model figured out, we decided it was time to expand. From 1999 to 2003 we went through a period of national expansion that resulted in adding operations in forty states and tripling in size four years in a row.

"Revenue increased from a million dollars a year to a couple hundred million a year, while employees grew from a few dozen to a few thousand. Meanwhile, our people became employee-owners of 40 percent of the company through an employee stock ownership plan (ESOP). Originally, the people in our little hometown barely knew who we were; after twelve years we suddenly became one of those 'overnight success stories.'

"More than any other accomplishment in our corporate history, my family, my executives, and my former employee-owners are proud of the mission statement that inspired our goals and the six core ideologies that guided our daily actions. From our first day to our very last, the company and its people were committed to working with compassion and integrity. We had compliance procedures and policies that were better than any other Medicare supplier in the country, and we were committed to becoming the 'gold standard' in that field. We were big and growing fast, so we knew the day would come when Medicare would want to check out every little detail. Sadly, when we fast-forward another twelve years, The SCOOTER Store came to an abrupt, tragic, and absurdly frustrating end.

"My belief in the values of our country made me too naïve to properly prepare for being attacked by one of our nation's largest bureaucracies. It clearly didn't help that we had also sued Medicare more than once to force it to follow its own rules. Once Medicare decided that it didn't want us around, it went to extraordinary lengths to put us out of business."

MEDICARE-BASED REVENUE

Doug continued, "Nearly 100 percent of our customers were over the age of sixty-five, which means that they were unavoidably insured by Medicare. When we first started the company, we only wanted to sell directly to the customer for cash. We didn't want to have to deal with Medicare. However, if you sell a product that is covered by Medicare to a Medicare beneficiary, you are legally required to file a Medicare claim.

"Medicare has a long history of being horribly abused by all kinds of fraud. It also has a history of being one of the biggest, clumsiest, and most irrational bureaucracies in the federal government. That is why we didn't want to work with it, but we were committed to helping our customers regain their personal mobility, so we were stuck with dealing with Medicare."

Doug explained that Medicare fraud primarily comes in three forms:
1. Medicare is billed for items that were never delivered.
2. Medicare is billed for a more expensive item than the patient actually received.
3. Medicare is billed for an item that does not meet Medicare's medical-necessity criteria.

He went on, "There are plenty of determined crooks who rip off Medicare and taxpayers under the first two items. It is the third item—medical necessity—that can be difficult for even the most honest companies. As defined by federal law, medical necessity must be determined by the patient's doctor. If the doctor sends a valid prescription and order to a Medicare supplier, the supplier is obligated to fulfill it. Most suppliers don't have doctors on staff, and even if they did, those doctors are not allowed to make the medical-necessity determination.

"Fortunately (we thought), Medicare went to Congress in 1994 and created a process to certify medical necessity for medical equipment. Medicare created a form and had Congress amend the Social Security Act to say that suppliers could use 'Certificates of Medical Necessity,' signed and sworn to by the patient's doctor, to demonstrate that the item ordered by the doctor was medically necessary. Problem solved—right? Yes, for a short time.

"On September 21, 1999, just as we were beginning our national expansion, Medicare kicked out every single one of The SCOOTER

Store's claims on the same day, stating that we had 'failed to certify the medical necessity' of those claims.

"'No problem,' we said. 'We have a valid Certificate of Medical Necessity, signed and sworn to by the patients' doctors for every single claim.'

"'No,' said Medicare, 'that's just a piece of paper called a CMN—it doesn't certify medical necessity.'

"My dad and I flew to Washington, DC, and we called on every senator from the five states in which we were doing business. We were going to run out of cash within days if something didn't change. Miraculously, we were able to convince Medicare to change course and pay us for all of our claims. Medicare *hates* being called by US senators.

"The good news was that we got paid for all those September 1999 claims. The bad news is that Medicare continued to insist that their own, congressionally defined Certificate of Medical Necessity did not certify medical necessity.

"Over the next few years, Medicare would ask to audit thirty claims at a time from many of our growing number of locations across the United States. The audit results were almost always identical; they would deny nearly 100 percent of the sample claims because we had 'failed to certify medical necessity,' and they would demand repayment. Then, they would take the 80 or 90 percent 'error rate' and extrapolate that to all claims from that location for the prior year and demand immediate repayment.

"We appealed all of the denied claims," Doug continued, "and won payment on almost all of them. We were spending $4,000-$5,000 per claim in legal fees to collect $4,000. It was a disaster. Medicare routinely told us that there was no precedent-setting federal court decision to define the Certificate of Medical Necessity despite its new definition in the Social Security Act, so they could do whatever they wanted. We decided to take a batch of claims to federal court to ask for judgment. We had to wait until Medicare denied a batch of claims, appeal the denial, and then we were allowed to sue in federal court.

"We filed our lawsuit in 2003 and began a four-and-a-half–year legal battle with the same bureaucracy responsible for 90 percent of our revenue. The federal government countersued and sent the FBI to Texas to investigate, harass, and terrify my employee-owners. To say that they made life a living hell for us would be an understatement.

"By 2007 we had won payment on almost all claims denied in these foolish audits. Medicare never changed the definition and never eliminated the authority of a Certificate of Medical Necessity in the Social Security Act, but it did change its internal policy for scooter and power wheelchairs to specify that it would no longer use Certificates of Medical Necessity for those items. In other words, even if we did win our lawsuit, it wouldn't matter because the certificates were no longer used for our products.

"We still wanted our day in court. However, with only a few weeks to go before trial, the federal attorneys asked the judge for a three-year delay to 'collect more data.' Our ordeal had nearly killed the company, as we shrank from $600 million per year to less than $200 million.

"Medicare was making numerous rule changes, and even though we were the largest supplier in our industry, we were excluded from working with Medicare on those changes because we were suing each other. They simply refused to talk to us. I couldn't see us lasting another three years. We agreed to settle our suit against Medicare and their counter-suit against us; we agreed to a five-year Corporate Integrity Agreement that included an annual audit of 250 claims by an Independent Review Organization (IRO). Other than that, Medicare did not ask us to change a single operating practice. I was excited that we could get back to business as usual. My excitement didn't last long.

"During the several years of this legal battle," Doug explained, "Medicare tried multiple ways to change the rules. One of those attempts was a new program called PECOS, which was a critical part in the perfect storm that finally pushed The SCOOTER Store off the edge— more on that later. Another attack came in the form of a radically redefined and restricted medical-necessity criteria. Medicare had the audacity to call it a clarification of its long-standing policy. Under the 'clarification,' if a patient could take only one step, he or she was considered ambulatory and not qualified for any type of mobility equipment, including a cane, walker, or crutch. Patients who could walk one step, but no more, would be left imprisoned in their beds, unable to go to the bathroom or move around the house.

"We led the industry to fight that change, and Medicare finally backed off, saying that the suppliers misunderstood. Yeah, right! Medicare also went through several arbitrary and irrational calculations to justify major price reductions, and we saw our average revenue per unit drop by about 60 percent . . . sixty percent! Those changes were devastating to us, but it was even more devastating to our competitors. Still we found a way to survive and grow unit volume."

AN "INDEPENDENT" AUDIT

Doug said, "In our 2007 Corporate Integrity Agreement, we were required to hire an IRO to review 250 claims each year for five years. The terms of the audit were well defined, and, again, I optimistically believed that we could make this work out. We hired Navigant, the largest IRO in the country.

"The Navigant review came up with a 2 to 3 percent error rate. We actually had the chance to challenge those results, because Navigant had miscalculated; the error rate should have been much lower. However, our lawyers advised against pursing that challenge, because they said Medicare wouldn't like the extremely low error rate. I guess they were right.

"In 2010 Medicare's inspector general told us that they were going to fire Navigant because they didn't like the results of the audits. Navigant had never been removed from a corporate integrity audit in its history, and no other IRO in the United States would then accept the contract because of the terms that Medicare wanted to stipulate. Although the IRO is supposed to conduct an independent audit, Medicare wanted to dictate extreme terms. As a result, we were not able to find another IRO until nearly the end of the fourth year.

"Once it eliminated Certificates of Medical Necessity for scooters and power wheelchairs, Medicare went through several versions of what would be required for new medical-necessity documentation. When we started the year-four audit, Medicare insisted that the new IRO apply the latest documentation standards to claims generated before those standards were developed. The result was predictable (and predetermined, in my opinion). The IRO generated a substantially higher error rate, and Medicare demanded immediate repayment. To be clear, the IRO did *not* determine that our customers lacked medical need for the equipment, just that our documentation didn't fit the documentation standards that had been developed *after* those claims were filed.

"For example, Medicare wanted the doctors' paperwork to state exactly how far the patient could walk without assistance. If the paper-work didn't have that answer specified in exact number of feet, the claim was denied.

"By this time," Doug went on, "The SCOOTER Store had been forced to bring in a private equity company, Sun Capital in Boca Raton, Florida, to fund working capital because of another Obamacare-initiated rule change. Deb Taylor, the CFO of Medicare, told our private equity company that she would work something out with Sun Capital if the board agreed to remove me as CEO. Otherwise she would cancel our Medicare supplier number, putting us out of business immediately. As chairman of the board, I still had control of the company, but my choice was either to fire myself or watch the company die. I chose to step aside and hope for the best. It didn't work out well. Deb Taylor canceled our Medicare number, and The SCOOTER Store died."

THE FBI STEPS IN

Doug wanted to share one more story: "Medicare added a program for doctors called PECOS. Doctors who did *not* enroll in the PECOS program were no longer allowed to order any type of medical equipment, including scooters and power wheelchairs. However, on the day the program officially launched, there were two huge problems: First, four out of every five doctors in the United States were not enrolled, and second, there was no way to look up which doctors were enrolled and which were not.

"Medicare said that suppliers should simply keep on accepting orders from all doctors. Later, Medicare, at its own discretion, might or might not look back to the start date and deny claims ordered by any doctor who was not in PECOS.

"Since The SCOOTER Store accepted orders from doctors all over the country, this new rule meant that 80 percent of those orders were now from disqualified doctors—and there was no way to tell which doctors were which. We had already lived through years of Medicare audits and their extrapolated repayment demands. We were not going to do that again. Because we had committed to be the gold standard of Medicare suppliers—and Medicare didn't want us to accept orders from certain doctors—we were determined to find a way to make that happen.

"The SCOOTER Store worked with a Medicare contractor to obtain legal access to the enrolled-doctor list, and we created our own database that labeled doctors as red or green—red if they were *not* in PECOS (or banned from Medicare for other reasons), green if they were enrolled. This was difficult to enforce because 80 percent of all Medicare beneficiaries in the country were seeing doctors who were not in PECOS. We had to convince our prospective customers to find a doctor who was enrolled. Fortunately, many of our customers saw many doctors, and we could locate another one for them whom they already knew. Many customers, however, had to find a new physician. It was a mess.

"In 2013, after Medicare had blackmailed me into leaving my company, and new private equity partners were running the business, more than 150 FBI agents showed up in New Braunfels to raid our headquarters building. The FBI and Department of Justice have never officially said what they were investigating, but the end result was very clear. Our bankers no longer wanted to fund our working capital, and our private equity partners wanted out at all costs.

"So, what was the FBI investigating?" Doug said, "Their primary focus seemed to be that they heard we had a red/green doctor list, and they heard we were sending Medicare beneficiaries to doctors that the patients had never seen before. They were pretty sure that meant something criminal was going on. (The FBI and the Department of Justice clearly didn't communicate well with Medicare.)

"I would add this: Working with the federal government can be fun and rewarding. It can also be the most hurtful, frustrating, and disillusioning thing you will ever experience. The government can outlast and outspend you. Nameless, faceless career bureaucrats who run huge bureaucracies like Medicare have their own rules.

"So proceed with caution. Even if you do everything right, it can change the rules, apply them retroactively, and punish you. The FBI and DOJ have the right to harass, intimidate, and lie to anyone. In my opinion, the agencies have been evil, vindictive, and un-American to my employee-owners and the customers we serve. Their foolish lack of knowledge, combined with their desire to have a trophy to mount on the wall, led them to put thousands of people out of work, destroy the enterprise that my family spent decades building, erase my personal equity in the company, and, worst of all, virtually remove powered mobility devices as an option for elderly disabled people. The SCOOTER Store sold to more than 50 percent of the US market. Since our departure, the market has collapsed to less than 10 percent of what it was."

Doug's story is a cautionary tale. His equity in The SCOOTER Store went from $200 million to nothing virtually overnight. Luckily, he had taken some chips off the table through the years; he and his family are still comfortable, although 90 percent or more of their estate evaporated.

AN INTERNATIONAL CONSTRUCTION DEAL

The next entrepreneur wanted his name and company to remain anonymous. We'll call him Don. He graduated as an African History major from Harvard, worked at JP Morgan on Wall Street, and later received his MBA from Wharton. Don is an incredibly sharp go-getter.

An African History major from Harvard with an MBA from Wharton, this anonymous entrepreneur was CEO of a construction-equipment company that went bankrupt. Though he personally lost almost everything, within a few years he was able to sell 80 percent of his company for $60 million. YPO member.

Don said, "In the early '90s, when I didn't have much money, I did an acquisition of about $4 million to buy the business that I had been running. It consisted of more or less half a million dollars of equity. My two sisters and my dad participated, and I got a complicated finance structure of debt, some from the state of Pennsylvania and some from the city of Philadelphia. I also leveraged some real estate. It was a bootstrap leverage-finance deal, typical for the time.

"I was stupid to do the deal. I should have looked elsewhere, but I did what I knew, and we were off and running. Four years later, after a lot of work, we succeeded in getting the biggest deal we ever set up—a $50 million contract with a foreign government for some construction equipment.

"After that foreign government collapsed—it had a parliamentary system—there were elections, and a new coalition came in. There were new ministers for transportation: one for air, one for land, and one for sea. I remember our agent calling me up and saying that this was really good news because of the three ministers appointed, one was his roommate in college and the other was his partner's roommate in college. The third guy we didn't know, but we had a two-out-of-three chance that we were going to have a good relationship with whomever it was."

BLACKMAIL OR EXTORTION?

Don continued, "Well, as the odds worked out, the third guy, the new minister of sea navigation, was the one responsible for our contract. He was a corrupt politician whose background was in the garbage-truck industry. Sure enough, this guy asked for a meeting.

"'You've got a $50 million contract,' the minister told us. 'So we're going to cancel it unless you do the following: Give me a million dollars and then hire my cousin to do a big piece of work.'

"'Are you kidding?' I asked.

"'No, I'm not,' he said.

"'Well, I can't do that. You're crazy,' I said.

"'Well, you'll see what happens,' he responded.

"That exchange precipitated a rather ugly war. This was a very big deal for our company. We had financing for the $50 million. The working capital financing was through Exim Bank, an independent US-insured government agency whose job is to promote foreign exports. Exim Bank still exists, and I use it today.

"We told Exim Bank we had a problem, but they responded that they had defaults that were much bigger than ours. There were foreign companies who owed them $500 million within that same country alone, so frankly they didn't care about the $2 million that we owed them. They told us to figure it out and tell them how we solved it."

CASH CRUNCH

"Starting in 1998," Don remembered, "we were working on this contract, but the government started paying us late in retaliation for not agreeing to the extortion that the minister requested. We were quite open with our bank. Because the foreign government paid us late, we were not able to sustain the big hiccups: The late payments put us in trouble with our vendors immediately, and we defaulted on various contracts. This forced us to use a shipyard in Miami to do part of the work, while the foreign government gave us problems all along the way. Our relationship became a horrible dance where we started using advance payments from other newer projects to pay past ones.

"I talked to our bank and let them know we were having challenges. I had no extra outside source of money to put into it; I actually owed my dad half a million dollars. Then our Hartford, Connecticut, bank said, 'We think our outside counsel can solve your problems.' So I took our banker's lawyer to meet with officials in the foreign country, but he couldn't do anything to help.

"We became a workout case [what a lender calls a borrower who is having problems], and we were still doing business with other people and still producing some products. But now we were starting to have severe shortages. The pool of vendors and customers who realized we had problems kept getting bigger.

"Throughout this time, the bank maintained faith in my efforts, energy, and intentions. But then the foreign government kept changing. We would come up with some preliminary agreement, the government would change, and we had to start at ground zero. Time is money, and this was really killing us, yet the foreign government couldn't really acknowledge that it was its own corruption that had started the problem in the first place.

"By the early 2000s we were starting to look for people to buy the business and actually found two different buyers. The first went away because

Exim didn't respond in a timely fashion to give the buyer approval to buy the business. The second buyer got in trouble after 9/11.

"At this point I'd been married for eighteen years. Then I found out that my wife was having an affair, and the distraction of my business challenges was not helping things. She was not an owner of the business, and she was not responsible for my debts, which was important. She did have some assets of her own, but as part of the divorce process, I had to represent that my company wasn't worth anything. If it was worth more subsequently, she had the right to reopen things.

"In 2001 my dad got sick with leukemia. He was sort of my partner, though I wasn't borrowing more money from him nor was I asking him to sustain any of my problems. Still, it was painful for him to watch my divorce and business difficulties. He died on his eightieth birthday, right before 9/11.

"Both my controller and my COO still had faith that there would be a positive outcome in the business. We took turns financing the company payroll personally, waiting for some check or some other piece of business to come in. Our business was doing, maybe, $15 million a year beyond the $50 million contract. We had about one hundred employees in our Philadelphia plant, and we had a related business in the Midwest that had about twenty-five people. They were separate legally, but I was a majority owner of each business, and both were suffering.

"Right after 9/11, I called my banker to say that I thought the business would die, it was just a question of when. Under certain terms and conditions, I thought I could make an offer to buy out the company with the last piece of real estate I had left. He told me to go ahead.

"Of course, my bank hired a third party to do due diligence. It's an interesting experience; Banks come in and look in your drawers to make sure you're clean. There was a favorable outcome to that investigation, but it was still humiliating. At least I was grateful that I'd done things the right way."

OFFER AND COMPROMISE

"I sat down with the CEO of the private-sector bank," Don continued, "and we agreed that the business was going to die. I was the personal guarantor—illiquid and insolvent. I wanted to help the bank minimize its losses as well as mine, but I needed to know the bank wouldn't shoot me in the end and put me in a personal bankruptcy.

"So we worked out a deal called an offer and compromise. We would try to liquidate the inventory and other assets and realize certain outcomes. In the end, I would not be held personally accountable beyond certain pledged assets, and they would not proceed further.

"We worked out a deal with the bank in principle, then we had to work out a deal with Exim Bank—the principal secured lender, the guarantor—because they were going to take a hit, too. In February, I called a board member of Exim Bank, said we had an agreement with the private bank, and asked to talk to somebody there to see if we could work out a deal.

"He said, 'I'll set up a meeting for you with the Exim Bank CFO.'

"I met with the CFO of Exim Bank in Washington, DC, and reviewed the deal. The CFO agreed that if I used my remaining assets in accordance with what I'd negotiated with the private bank, that Exim Bank wouldn't go after me for any shortfall. We shook hands on the agreement, and I completed the deal with the private bank, knowing that after doing my best I wouldn't have any personal liability beyond that which I'd agreed to.

"With the help of a sharp attorney, we started a new firm with a related name and methodically transferred to it the old business and employees. In the process, we were able to shed many liabilities—a labor union, huge accounts payables, and environmental issues associated with the former hundred-year-old company.

"That all took place in 2003. By then I was divorced and had a new girlfriend. We signed a contract on a house in Philadelphia, and the very next week a debt collection agency called me to say that I owed the US government $12 million. I explained that I had an agreement with a private-sector bank and Exim Bank that I would not be held personally accountable beyond my pledged assets. They replied, 'We don't know anything about that.'"

US GOVERNMENT EXTORTION

Don continued, "I called up the chief financial officer of Exim Bank. 'Six weeks ago,' I said, 'I sat in your office, and we discussed this deal. Why am I getting called from a debt collection agency?'

"'I don't remember that meeting,' the guy says.

"'You're kidding,' I said.

"'No,' he responded. 'I don't remember the meeting.'

"'Well, it's pretty damn important to me,' I said.

"I got hold of the chief lawyer who had been involved in this for the US government and told her, 'We have this written agreement that your signature is on. We have an offer and compromise. So what is this about?'

"'Well, first of all I would deny that there is such an agreement,' she said.

"'You're kidding me.'

"'No,' she said.

"'Well, I have your signature on this thing,' I said.

"'If you establish that there is such an agreement,' she said, 'I will deny that it means anything.' And then she said, 'By the way, what's your budget for a legal defense? Mine is unlimited.'

"I concluded that she must have thought I'd gotten away with something and intended to put me out of business and in personal bankruptcy. Horrified, I called up the private bank and spoke with the outside counsel. 'What the hell is this about?' I asked.

"The counsel replied, 'You know, this is terrible. We're sorry. Let's see what we can do, and we'll let you know.'

"Then a couple of months later, it all went away. I had no clarification of what had taken place, but the collection agency stopped calling me.

"Finally, a weird thing happened: I was on my to a Harvard-Yale football game in New Haven. I flew into Hartford, and by chance, I passed the office for the private bank counsel. I had never been to his office before, but I stopped by.

"'How are you doing?' I asked. 'I had this problem that was horrible. Then it seemed to go away—but I don't understand what happened.'

"'I want to show you something,' he said. He handed me a letter that he had written to Exim Bank in response to the request from the bank and the collection agency for him to act as a witness against me. The letter said something like, 'Dear Exim Bank, I understand you're trying to go after our customer for his personal guarantee. This is absolutely egregious and outrageous. It is not only acting in bad faith, but it is clearly against what you've agreed to do. However, the point is that the biggest problem we have from the outcome of this transaction is that you, Exim Bank, liquidated the equipment bought for a foreign country. You sold the equipment to third parties, and the biggest risk we have is that their government will come after us for doing this. We need our customer as a potential witness and support in such a case, if such a case should arise. It is highly predictable that it might. So get lost.'

"That letter saved my ass, because the collection agency realized that even though Exim Bank was its client, they had no case and no reason to pursue it. That letter forced the US government to back off. I had cleared that obstacle, but I was still horrified. To think that there are people working for the US government who have personal agendas and who are willing to use the resources of the government for their own use was pretty shocking."

It seems incredible that this entrepreneur could make it through all of the problems he faced, but Don relentlessly persevered through massive challenges and losses. In November 2009 he sold 80 percent of his successor company for much more than $25 million, married his girlfriend, and today continues to work as CEO for the company's new owners.

A BANKER'S PERSPECTIVE

It's useful to hear from Gary Votapka, a founder and CEO of Mission Oaks Bank in Temecula, California. Early in his career, he was an FDIC examiner. His view of the government was this: "If you're working in a regulated industry, you have no friends in the government." He noted that you might start out with some kind of a relationship, but if an adverse situation arises and positions harden, things can become surreal. "Don't expect to find any of the good rapport you had when times were good."

In 2011, Gary was levied a personal $5,000 civil penalty to reinforce the government's desire to see him leave his CEO position of the bank that he founded.

"You have to conduct yourself in such a way that you don't have personal exposure," Gary went on. "When a bank fails, it's almost standard procedure that the regulators sue the directors and executive management. Regulators want to take money away from directors and executives, so they can go after the bank's D&O insurance. It can be freaky when you realize the US government that you know files suit against you. You realize there's just no way you have the same resources they have."

LESSONS LEARNED

- When times are good, doing business with the government is great. When times are bad, doing business with the government can get out of control.

- Personal relationship dynamics can make or break the government's reaction.

- In litigation, businesses watch their budgets and resolve conflicts cost effectively. Government entities respond differently, apparently pursuing vendettas. Government employees have no personal "skin in the game."

- If entrepreneurs have problems with one government agency, those problems can also involve other government agencies, compounding the issues.

- When businesses have issues with the government, colleagues, friends, and family often believe that the business is at fault. After all, the government is always right, fair, and good, isn't it?

CHAPTER 7

EXTERNAL EVENTS

*"No matter how good a company or individuals
believe themselves to be, half of all decisions
made each and every day are wrong."*

Unpredictable external events affect business. The impact of onetime events such as Y2K, 9/11, and the Great Recession can't be known at the time they occur, and that makes decision making more like a game of chance.

In the early 1990s I participated in the three-year Massachusetts Institute of Technology Birthing of Giants program organized by Verne Harnish. (Verne was also the founder of the Entrepreneurs' Organization, or EO.) During the program, Verne had two powerful and tough CEOs talk to us. One headed the second largest software company in the world; the other was the CEO of the restaurant Boston Market. They explained that no matter how good a company or individuals believe themselves to be, half of all decisions made each and every day are wrong, whether the organization is General Electric, the White House, or your neighborhood pizza shop.

The takeaway from their presentations was this: You need to identify the decisions that have the ability to kill you and focus on those. You want to make sure you fare better than 50 percent on those few decisions. This may sound easy, but it is harder than you imagine. There have been numerous times when I was well aware that a decision I was about to make was critical. Yet, in hindsight, it's clear I chose the wrong path, and there were horrible consequences.

EMPLOYEE LEASING

Brian Lesk is a smart, scrappy serial entrepreneur. From real estate to restaurants to employee leasing (outsourcing departments or functions), he chased opportunities and prospered. Around 1995 he started his employee-leasing business with the objective of being the biggest and the best. The industry was booming, but it had some irresponsible companies, including notorious ones that were not paying employment taxes. Brian set out to be the impeccable and dependable national player in that space. After about five years his company had about 15,000 people on the payroll every week, for an annual payroll of about $250 million. He was rolling!

Brian Lesk graduated from the University of Arizona. As CEO of an employee leasing company, Diversified Human Resources, located in Scottsdale, Arizona, he grew it to be worth about $75 million.

"We grew rapidly through the late '90s," Brian said. "There were very few regulations, which I thought was bad for the industry, because there were many companies that weren't running right; they were stealing tax and benefits money and creating a black eye on what was a really cool emerging industry. Those of us who were running right were using the existing tax and benefit laws to create very lucrative businesses. It was great because the business generated revenue with each payroll, and every time someone got a raise, we made a small percentage of that. Companies were expanding, and ours was a perfect service for them, because they could do tax payments and benefit administration in ten different states but manage it from one central location. We were growing at the right time."

Y2K

"I'll tell you about the first implosion," Brian went on. "Businesses were just starting to use computers, and everyone was freaking out about Y2K. I was a cheerleader for technology. Because of our industry, we were early computer-technology users. I wanted to make use of software and computers so that we could leverage our back office to create more profits. However, there's also a downside to technology. It doesn't always work, especially early on.

"We were growing, making lots of profit only two or three years in. We were hiring people and opening additional offices. I started to explore the potential of going public. One of our competitors, the biggest employee-leasing company, was purchased at the time for about $250 million dollars, and we were approaching that size.

"I went out and consulted all the experts. The experts said get a CFO, get a CTO, start to build the infrastructure, and get audited financials. So I did all the right things. I was going to find guys smarter than me.

"Back then, it was hard to find people who had any significant amount of technology experience, and when you found them they could call themselves whatever they wanted—god of technology . . . emperor of technology. I thought I'd found one of those guys, and I brought him in as a CTO. Those hires—the CTO and CFO—upended my organization because both of them had salary and equity demands that were greater than some of the people who had been with me from the very beginning."

The experts Brian hired convinced him that Y2K was going to bring the company down, if they didn't invest in the best hardware and all new leading-edge software. Up to this point Brian had been financing the company's growth himself. He began selling property, stocks, and anything he could to generate the cash needed to invest in these systems—about $1 million.

A MAGIC BULLET—TO THE HEAD

Brian continued, "Needless to say, all the new systems were implemented in time for Y2K, with a huge investment of time, energy, and money. January 2000 came, and all the payrolls were wrong. The system that they converted to had miscalculated, and the employees were pissed. People were calling us and saying their mortgage was due, they were losing their houses. It was about as bad as you can possibly get.

"I was taking every penny that I had and throwing it into this bottomless pit. I should have bankrupted the company. I was very wealthy at the time. I could have walked away. But I used every means available to stay alive. I was just too stubborn to quit.

"Every great entrepreneur who makes it has stood at the precipice, ready to jump. In many cases I don't know why they don't. I don't know why I didn't walk away. I had a company that was arguably worth $75 million bucks. That wasn't my number—that was a number the CFO was negotiating with investment bankers. Overnight, it was literally worth nothing. Matter of fact, it was negative.

"We took the new software out, and we went back to the original software. The CTO told me there was absolutely no way it would work. Yet it worked just fine. So we migrated everything back. But in two and a half weeks we'd lost about 65 percent of our clients."

TURNAROUND MANAGERS

Dan Stephenson is the CEO of Rancon Real Estate and an experienced land developer in Southern California with a laser focus and a well-honed regional concentration. He is a master at managing investors and a dynamic and engaging man. He is the ultimate positive thinker.

Dan Stephenson was an undergraduate at the University of Southern California, and he attended the Harvard executive MBA program. He is the founder and CEO of Rancon Real Estate in California. As a successful longtime developer, he's been through many recessions, accumulating as much as $200 million in assets. YPO member.

Dan talked about two of the many recessions he's been through: "The one thing I did do in the recessions of the 1980s, and then again in the early '90s, is I brought in a very cold-blooded turnaround manager. I don't mean cold-blooded in a negative manner. His attitude was that you cannot have Christmas parties, you cannot have fun, you cannot have incentive trips—all the things I normally did. This manager said that in a recession you couldn't do any of that stuff. He had the guts to lay off a lot people when I couldn't. The good news was that I was smart enough to realize I needed to hire someone who had the ability to manage in a recession and then to step aside.

"We weathered the storm. I think we went down to two people in my corporate division—from one hundred to two. The manager is the only one who came out ahead, but he saved the company. If he hadn't done it, frankly I'd have run us into oblivion."

THE COMEBACK AND THE GREAT RECESSION

Dan continued, "In the '90s, I was lucky enough to buy a $300 million portfolio from the Resolution Trust Corporation at twenty cents on a dollar, and we made our investors eleven times their money. That investment got me back on my feet.

"As the market came back, I acquired a lot of assets, and by 2006 I was up to $200 million in net worth—$20 million liquid. I had learned an awful lot from the prior recessions. I'd diversified into income-producing real estate, so I was not strictly dependent upon our real estate company or the assets, which by then were primarily land. I was comfortable; I had written a book, had done seminars on how to be recession-proof, and had done all the things that I felt I should have done.

"Two things are interesting about the Great Recession: Number one, $20 million of liquidity wasn't enough in hindsight, because I had done more leverage than I should have, much of it on undeveloped land. Several other loans were for the construction of retail projects.

"My greatest exposure was a new 313,000-square-foot retail center we developed. All of a sudden, when my construction loan came due, I was not able to refinance it. All the construction was completed, and I had it leased to a lot of tenants. Unfortunately, four of them went bankrupt, including Levitt's Furniture and Party City. When it became time for me to replace my construction loan, there was nothing there.

"I had personally guaranteed about $7.5 million of my $65 million loan, but I also had $10 million in cash invested in the project. It was worth about $95 million before the market crashed. The bank ended up letting me off my guarantee as long as I allowed them to sell it. It sold for far less than its value, wiping out all of my equity.

"The shame of it was that I was actually covering my debt service on the $65 million loan. They were getting the interest from me; we were managing the asset magnificently, but they didn't care. They just wanted to get out of the debt, and, unfortunately, I was the fall guy. So I lost my $30 million of equity and probably more importantly, I lost my $10 million in cash."

OFFSHORE INSURANCE

"I had set up an insurance company that we funded with $4 million," Dan said. "That was actually enough for us to borrow from to buy real estate. During the recession—from 2007 to, say, 2012—I was able to borrow money to buy property and then turn around and resyndicate that property.

"During a recession, there is no bank money for land. But to get bargains, you need to close escrow the day someone calls and says, 'Hey, we want to sell it.' Because of the $4 million of available cash, we could make an offer, give deposit dollars the next day, and close thirty days later. We were buying real estate at ten to fifteen cents on the dollar.

"That was how I approached the fact that we were underwater. We'd lost all of our net worth. If you look at the guarantees, we had *negative* net worth, which seems hard to believe when you're starting with $200 million. But the bottom line is that land is the first thing to go down in a recession and the last thing to go up in a rising market, so your net worth is very volatile, too. Sort of like the old saying, 'You live poor and die rich.' In the real estate land business, it's so."

LESSONS LEARNED

- Half of all the decisions made by your company are wrong. It's important to discern which decisions are important enough to kill you. Focus on those, and get them right.

- Avoid ultra-risky, so-called bleeding-edge technologies for systems that you must rely on.

CHAPTER 8

SOMETIMES IT'S JUST PLAIN BAD LUCK

"I'm a forge-ahead kind of guy, a positive,
glass-half-full rather than half-empty guy.
I just try to do the best I can."

Sometimes events occur that can take down the most careful and thoughtful of entrepreneurs. As I show in this chapter, sometimes you just have just bad luck.

It's rare, but it does happen. On the high seas, it's called the perfect storm. In business, there have been plenty of uncontrolled variables that seemed to be totally unpredictable. As I noted in the previous chapter, Y2K, 9/11, and even the Great Recession are examples of events with unforeseen impacts on business. What follows are the stories of a software CEO and a home builder. Both are wonderfully successful businessmen; when their businesses failed, they landed on their feet, running.

Gary Greenberg is a dyed-in-the-wool entrepreneur. His story proves that there is a great deal of luck required to grow a business and accumulate wealth. He had decades of success, but incidents of just plain bad luck threw him off the rails. However, his spirit and positive outlook never faded.

Gary Greenberg was raised in Chicago and graduated from the University of Oklahoma. He focused on the food-distribution business and sold his first company to Kraft Foods for $20 million. His second company, SAGE Enterprises, grew to $400 million in sales with 400 employees. His outside investments were largely with Bernard Madoff. YPO member.

Gary said, "Growing up in the mid-sixties, all I ever wanted was my own business. I was a caddie at a well-known country club in Chicago, and there were a lot of wealthy guys there. I wanted to be one of those guys. I wanted to be a member at that country club, and I wanted to be in my own business."

A TOUGH CHILDHOOD

Four events affected Gary's life and set the course for his career and future. He described them: "Number one, I pretty much grew up as a juvenile delinquent in Chicago. I was from a middle-class neighborhood but got in with the wrong kids. I was at the police station several times between the ages of eleven and thirteen, and my parents were really beside themselves.

"Two, as a result of my juvenile delinquency, I was not a great student. I was a very good athlete growing up so, when I wasn't creating havoc, I spent most of my time on the sports field, playing basketball, baseball, and football.

"Consequently, I was going to try to play baseball in college. I ended up going to the University of Oklahoma, which was a fair academic school. It was a school that I could get into and one where, maybe, I could walk on and play baseball. I went there from 1965 through

1969. But in 1967, while out on a fraternity 'walkout' in Fort Worth, Texas, I got shot in the back. The bullet lodged in my heart. Although in the mid-sixties heart-lung machines and heart surgery weren't that advanced, I actually was able to survive. I was nineteen years old and was in the hospital in the critical-care or intensive-care units for almost two months.

"I didn't see it at the time, but that was a life-changing incident. All I wanted to do was get back on the baseball field, and I really didn't care about too much else. I thought they could just get the bullet out, cauterize my wound, and I'd be out of there. It didn't work that way, and in retrospect it was probably quite amazing. Several newspapers and medical articles at the time said I should not have lived."

HARD WORK AND LUCK—GOOD AND BAD

Gary continued, "Here's the third point: In 1971, when I was two years out of college, I was lucky to meet another guy, and we started our own business; we were in business for thirty-two years. In the fifteenth year, we sold the business to Kraft and made some money. I was lucky: I was a multimillionaire at thirty-nine years old.

"We sold the company for around $20 million, but we'd had about $8 or $9 million dollars of debt, so in 1986 we came away with $11 or $12 million, shared between the two of us. We also had a five-year contract, and I was trying to figure out what to do with the rest of my life. We ended up buying the company back, and we continued on with it from 1989 until 9/11. Our business distributed in-flight products of all different types to the airline industry: food, paper, plastics, disposable beverages, etcetera; however, 9/11 hurt us.

"In 2001 we were at a run rate of about $450 million with 400 employees and distribution centers all over the United States and throughout the world. After 9/11, we anticipated that our 2002 run rate would be slightly over $200 million, and it was. To make up the loss, we tried everything we could to restructure. We attempted to figure out what to do with our assets, other lines of business that we could move into, but the bottom line was our infrastructure was so large at that point that it was incredibly difficult to make up for $250 million of lost business and lost gross profits.

"The business was thrown into bankruptcy, and it was a very difficult time in my life. We liquidated that business at the end of 2002 and lost whatever equity we had in it, which for me was somewhere between $10 and $20 million.

"With the help of two YPO forums and other assistance, I was able to make it through. Before 9/11, I had been doing some succession planning; after thirty years in our business, I was ready for a break.

"I was on the way to moving out of the day-to-day activities. We were going to be involved in strategy and financing, and I had already laid some seeds for other careers. I had become a board director for a publicly held bank here in Chicago at the request of a YPO buddy. I also began to do some consulting for a real estate firm. I was off and running.

"Of course, after 9/11 I had to put both those new interests on hold. I only went back to those things after we lost the business by starting another career, a real estate consulting and financing business.

"Then the fourth life-changing event happened: Bernie Madoff got arrested. I had been an eighteen-year investor with him. For all practical purposes, I was probably 60 or 70 percent invested in Madoff and basically lost it all the next day, everything I thought I had for retirement."

In spite of experiencing financial devastation, Gary is fully engaged in his two new businesses and doing well. He was eventually able to recover most of his Madoff investment through the efforts of the trustee for the former investment firm, and today he enjoys a nice lifestyle.

Gary looked back at those life-changing events: "I don't think too much about it anymore. I'm a forge-ahead kind of guy, a positive, glass-half-full rather than half-empty guy. I just try to do the best I can. By reinventing myself and continuing to put myself in new situations, I now have two active things that I'm involved in, and they're both very exciting, educational, and challenging mentally."

THE PERFECT STORM: THE GREAT RECESSION

Our second CEO for this chapter, whom I'll call Richard, prefers anonymity out of concern for legal liability. Richard is a brilliant, award-winning home builder. He works hard, is disciplined, well educated, and serious about being the best. He talked about how the Great Recession hit his business incredibly hard and caused it to spiral out of control.

This anonymous entrepreneur earned a BS and MBA from San Diego State University and became CEO of a Southern California–based home-building company that had peak sales of $180 million with 140 employees. YPO member.

"I had financials in excess of $100 million," Richard said, "with about $35 to $40 million liquid; $180 million of revenue was our peak in 2005. We had 140 employees. I had diversified my real estate plan across the spectrum as far as categories of building—residential, commercial, industrial apartments, government contracting, and private contracting.

"Our strategy was that when the private sector went down, that we'd jump over to the public sector. We did that type of contingency planning to enable us to shift employees and intellectual capital. We modeled our capital structure very conservatively. There was $350 million of capital stock with less than 50 percent leverage.

"In real estate, investors look at potential risk, and by all benchmarks and indices it seemed like the Great Recession shouldn't be a big deal. So we modeled the 10 percent correction, we modeled the 15 percent correction, and we modeled the 20 percent correction. We didn't model a 50 percent correction, and as everyone knows, residential land fell by more than 50 percent. We were too heavy in inventory of land.

"The fatal flaw in our planning was twofold. Inventory was heavy because, to a certain degree, inventory and large land holdings had been a bragging right. I had a lot of pressure to hire top people, and they were not willing to leave some other major public company unless there was a long-term backlog. They need to see their future, and I got caught up in having to provide that career path, that leadership development, all those things that are all good things in themselves. What they don't talk to you about is the downside risk.

"You're absorbing all those risks. You're hearing it from multiple sources within your organization, over and over again. It comes from the marketing department, from the finance department, and from the manufacturing department. They are all coming to you telling you the same thing, that you to have the best talent. You just kind of go along with it, and there's no pulling out of this scenario."

LESSONS LEARNED

- Have a broadly diverse investment portfolio. If you have a liquidity event through a sale of equity, develop a diverse portfolio. If the sale is a stock swap, liquidate methodically as soon as restrictions are lifted.

- In times of a revenue crisis, reduce overhead immediately.

- When the company is big enough, hire the best CFO feasible.

- Reduce personal spending when times are tough.

CHAPTER 9

FAILED ACQUISITIONS

"You've got to have the paranoid mentality
that you are always one step from death's door, and
you've got to operate the business accordingly."

Most acquisitions fail to perform as anticipated. Leading up to the dinner that celebrates closing the deal, both seller and buyer might be filled with grand visions and optimism, but one or two years later the results typically are underwhelming. Often the acquiring company really doesn't understand the key business drivers of the target company well enough. In this chapter, we explore those intricacies.

Brad Adams was the owner and CEO of a primarily automotive-based wire-stamping business. Appointed as CEO at age twenty-six, Brad knew the business well. He had recently bought an injection molding company, which offered more value to his customers through completed units.

Brad Adams holds a bachelor's degree from Occidental College and an MBA from Claremont College. He bought Solid State Stamping from his father's estate, and led the company as CEO for about twenty years, when he acquired an injection molding company. Both were located in California and at their peak had total combined revenues of $36 million. YPO member.

Brad recounted his story: "We bought a business that was right down the street. It was really the best candidate for doing insert molding, and we had talked about purchasing this company for years. One of the principals was a casual friend of mine. They'd wanted to sell for quite a while; however, we could never justify their asking price.

"We didn't do anything until 2007 when they were finally generating enough cash flow to justify their price."

MEZZANINE DEBT

"We commenced an acquisition," Brad continued, "and took on a very aggressive debt structure. We were actually past the tail end of the time when people were able to do those kinds of debt structures, but somehow we got it done anyway.

"I don't think you would do anything like that today. However, we had a senior lender who effectively put up about half of the purchase price, a mezzanine lender [a financier who specializes in higher-risk, second-lending positions] who put up another maybe 25 percent, a bridge lender who put in maybe another 15 percent, and then the sellers took back some cash as well. So all of the $18 million purchase price was debt; no cash was involved. It penciled out under all of our scenarios. We spent a lot of time doing sensitivity analysis at different levels of sales to make sure that we could get the debt repaid.

"But immediately after the closing on April 15, and for the month of May, the sales tanked, and the profits tanked even further. We were

90

trying to figure out what was going on. The gross profit by month for the previous four years had been about 20 to 22 percent. Every month it had been within that range. But our gross profit for May, for our first full month as owners, was 5 percent and the next month was 6 percent.

"We thought the first month might be a fluke, but it was real. I hired a forensic accountant to try to figure out what was going on. It turned out that the customer who had accounted for about half of the EBITDA stopped buying. Therefore, a fair amount of our overall revenue, but a disproportionate amount of the profits, disappeared."

DUE DILIGENCE

Brad continued, "In our industry it takes about a year and a half to two years for a customer to move its business. You don't just get up and say you're going to move to company X and do it. It's a pretty extensive process to design the tooling, design the processes, then get them built, debugged, and into manufacturing. We later found out this was something that had been in the works for about a year and a half; however, the previous owners had not disclosed the information to us. We had very extensive disclosures in the purchase agreement from the sellers about the customers, except the disclosures really missed the issue that the EBITDA was about to go away.

"By late spring of 2008—just two months after the closing—we were already limping along, in cash-flow trouble. Then the Great Recession hit. The combined businesses in 2007 did about $36 million in sales, but for the first twelve months after closing we did about $24 million. We were operating a $24 million company instead of a $36 million company, since the most profitable customer was no longer there. The sales continued to decline to about $18 million. This scenario was way outside the bounds of all the analysis we had done. We had not looked at any in which everything went wrong all at the same time.

"Then 2009 came along. We were 98 percent automotive. But because of the economy, the auto companies essentially shut down their plants for anywhere from three to six months to burn off inventories. The $18 million in revenue that seemed so low the previous year actually became attractive because in the first half of 2009 revenue was even worse. It was crisis management coming out of the gates. All the energy that we thought would go into building the business was really going into saving the business."

Brad and his team switched into survival mode. In 2010 they cut overhead and costs, so they were generating about $600,000 per month in EBITDA, and in spite of all the obstacles, they were still making it work. However, the abyss grew deeper.

The deathblow actually came on July 31, 2010. "In 2009 our big customers had started monitoring us," Brad recalled. "We were sending out financials, and they were spending a lot of time talking with our financial analyst, who was trying to convince them that we were going to survive.

"Finally one of our major customers decided to bring all their business in-house, and they had everything in place by September 2010.

"We limped along and kept the senior lender reasonably happy. We never missed any interest payments to him, and for the most part, we were able to make the principal payments. However, the rest of the debt structure was not getting anything: The mezzanine lender was getting accrued interest at a penalty rate of 18 to 20 percent against the $3.5 million dollar loan. The loan got up to about $6.5 million dollars as it kept accruing interest. The snowball kept getting bigger and bigger."

Nevertheless, Brad and his team kept the company alive and continued making payments.

"Then in February 2013," Brad said, "we decided that it was time to try and sell the business. We knew we weren't going to be able to repay all the debt, but hopefully we could get the first-position lender, Comerica, to take some sort of a discount to throw some money to the mezzanine lender and some to the bridge lender. We engaged a broker/investment banker who specializes in distressed businesses to find suitors for either debt or equity or both. That was progressing well. By early April, we had a number of suitors who were visiting, and we had finished site visits. We actually had one letter of intent, and we were anticipating a couple of others."

ILLOGICAL REACTIONS—INVOLUNTARY BANKRUPTCY

Brad went on, "And then I got a call from the mezzanine lender who said they were going to file a motion for involuntary bankruptcy against the business. It was just out of the blue and, strangely, by themselves, which isn't possible since you need three creditors to join together to file properly. They did it and left us wondering who the other two creditors were. It turned out there were no others.

"Why did the mezzanine lender force a bankruptcy filing? Nobody will ever know. We'd all been waiting for some grand strategy, because it looked like it was a suicide mission. They were putting themselves in a position to get nothing. It turned out it was just a stupid thing to do. It put the business in a very difficult situation.

"Because there was only one creditor, we could have contested the bankruptcy and easily gotten it dismissed. However, the genie was out of the bottle, and it was now a matter of public record. We proactively called our customers, because we knew they'd be calling us.

"For years, we'd been putting a lot of energy into putting on a good face with the marketplace. I think one of the amazing things is that for all of the decay behind the curtain in the business, the customers had no idea what was going on. Our deliveries were all on time, even though we had material shortage, and we had zero quality problems . . . literally zero.

"But as soon as the involuntary bankruptcy was filed, all the dirty laundry was out there for the world to see."

Ultimately, the company was sold in a bankruptcy sale.

THE IMPORTANCE OF DUE DILIGENCE

Brad mused on the chain of events: "I think the turning point in all this was the customer who pulled his business. The one area where I kicked myself was in our due diligence. This was the fourth biggest customer, and I had done personal due diligence on the top three. I did not do it on the fourth. Also, we didn't dig deep enough to realize how much profit was coming from this customer.

"It was a pretty insidious plot, and plot is the right word. I guess it's easy to see the plot now, because we know what we are looking for. It turned out the company we bought had gone to the customer about a year and a half before our acquisition and raised prices by 40 percent. The customer responded that they were not going to accept the increases and were going to move the business. The guy said fine. Therefore, for a whole year they had this extra 40 percent margin that was inflating the profits, and we didn't see it. We had no idea how much money was coming from this one customer.

"So part of the lesson, which is easier said than done, is just how important due diligence is. I saw it again when the company was sold through the bankruptcy. The acquiring company hired an accounting firm and said they'd done due diligence. They went through a rote sequence of analysis but probably didn't get at many of the issues.

"The learning point for me is that you really have to dig deep with due diligence; spend more time than you would like. Even if it isn't the most glamorous part of the job, it's a really important one.

"I was running a company as a turnaround for five years. I think I would be much more inclined to run a successful, healthy business as a turnaround now, because it creates energy in a situation where cash is tight, people are scared, and there's just so much going on. It takes energy to keep people engaged in the business. It's a tendency when times are good to ratchet the energy down. A turnaround mentality actually increases the energy you get from employees.

"One of the things I learned is you've got to have the paranoid mentality that you are always one step from death's door, and you've got to operate the business accordingly.

"The best policy is to be brutally honest, always. For the last five years, my approach with employees at all levels was to tell them everything—the good, the bad, and the ugly—and then tell them how we were going to deal with it together. I think they get accustomed to that, and once they're accustomed to it, they respond with, 'Here's a problem, and here's how we're going to deal with it.' Stability becomes less of an issue because they generate the confidence that, yeah, we've got problems, but we had problems before, and we know how to deal with it."

LESSONS LEARNED

- Understand the importance of not completely delegating due diligence to accounting firms during acquisitions. Pay close attention; be engaged.

- Understand that the vast majority of acquisitions vastly underperform expectations. Be careful to be realistic, not overly optimistic.

- If acquiring a firm, verify 80 percent of the revenue by contacting strategic customers.

- Understand the importance of communicating openly with employees, vendors, and clients through hard times. Communication builds trust.

- Run your company as a turnaround every day, even in good times. It keeps the energy up and generates creative problem solving.

CHAPTER 10

THE IMPORTANCE OF TEAM MEMBERS

"We knew the company was only as good as the people we hired, and we wanted the best for the role."

Having the right skills and experience on your team can make the difference between success and failure. Sometimes hiring people with the experience you need, however, can conflict with developing the culture you want for your company.

I have always been a big believer in the importance of corporate culture. My companies have tended toward strong cultures that we fostered and developed intentionally, and for decades I've hired people to fit into them.

CORPORATE CULTURE VERSUS WHAT YOU NEED

It's vital to have appropriate financial expertise on your management team. In my first company, MuniFinancial, I had acted as CEO and CFO, relying on strong controllers or accounting managers to handle the financials and tax preparation. With my second company,

TurnKey, it was obvious that once we hit $50 million in revenue with 100 percent annual growth we needed a CFO, one who was strong and experienced.

I had learned that careful recruiting was key for hiring leadership team members. We spent a couple of months recruiting highly experienced CFOs and narrowed the search down to two candidates. Steve was a CFO from the San Francisco Bay Area with about fifteen years of experience with high-growth construction companies. He had raised capital and helped with a successful sale of a company with pre-IPO preparation. His experience was perfect, but his manner was very direct and unrefined.

The second candidate, Phillip, was born and raised in Paris, had done his undergraduate and graduate work at top Ivy League schools, was a CPA from Price Waterhouse, and had fifteen years of experience with manufacturing. Phillip was refined and elegant and a pleasure to be with.

Part of the hiring process that I had implemented years earlier was extensive testing and interviewing. We conducted reasoning tests, work-style personality tests, background checks, and drug testing. Normally, we would require eight to ten interviews for each candidate before making an offer of employment. Included were extensive "360 interviews" with numerous people; the hiring manager conducted three separate interviews in different locations. For senior positions, we would typically have a dinner, preferably with spouses. We knew the company was only as good as the people we hired, and we wanted the best for the role.

Filling the CFO position was an incredibly difficult decision for us. In hindsight, we made a huge mistake. The accounting managers had interviewed both candidates and found Steve far too abrasive compared to Phillip. They felt Phillip reflected the sophistication and culture of the company and would be more pleasant to spend long days with. On the other hand, I pushed back and said that Steve's direct approach and experience would be a nice compliment to our team.

In the end, we hired Phillip. Perhaps I should have trusted my instincts. I have no doubt that this was one of several deadly mistakes I made as the CEO. I should have insisted on hiring Steve, even if it led to the resignation of a longtime accounting manager or controller. Steve would have forced the construction managers to maintain updated project financial information, would probably have had more accurate cash flow forecasts, and would have been less likely to spend our last remaining cash days before closing at the request of the nefarious private equity person.

Steve was also highly experienced with cash-flow-oriented entrepreneurial companies, whereas Phillip came from subsidiaries of larger enterprises that were more oriented to financial statements. For high-growth companies, it's all about cash flow, and projections take a lot of practice to get right.

A DIVERSITY OF STYLE AND SKILLS

Finally, an excellent management team needs diversity. Generally speaking, the more diversity the better. While I made extensive efforts to have diversity of sex and ethnicity on the management team, I was less successful bringing in employees who were different in style. TurnKey's co-founder and COO, Mike, was a brilliant team member from my MuniFinancial days. He was a fabulous colleague and highly competent but very similar to me in approach. I had an inspirational, anything's-possible, kick-ass style. My emphasis was rapid growth and building a truly world-class organization. Looking back, the company would have been better served with an experienced, hard-assed COO and CFO to help complement my style. Steve would have been a bottom-line, demanding CFO with a discipline that was lacking within the company.

According to two highly regarded bankruptcy attorneys, it is very common for entrepreneurs not to have qualified financial staff or, commonly, to disregard the advice given to them. These are frequently fatal flaws in companies that end up failing.

Jim Glazer, CEO of Elliott Manufacturing in Nebraska, almost lost his company in 2010 and 2011, perhaps, he said, because his CFO was merely acting as a controller. "We had accurate financials, but he did not help us in planning to get through the tough times," Jim said. "The guy we have now would be out front saying this is what needs to happen. Instead, we had me trying to figure out what we should do. I'm not smart enough to make all the calls."

LESSONS LEARNED

- In high-growth companies, you need top financial staff for your company.

- If you have a great financial team member on staff, listen to him or her! Their role is to cover the downside risks.

- Leadership teams need diversity in skill sets and approaches. Tough, demanding types have a role and purpose, especially when things get rough.

- If you're in a high-growth company, hire staff members who have that kind of experience.

- Listening to your team is crucial, but don't ignore your instincts.

PART THREE

FINANCING ISSUES

CHAPTER 11

PERSONAL GUARANTEES

*"Who made up the $50,000 a month
shortfall? I did."*

Personal guarantees are one of the most critical risk factors for entrepreneurs. While the use of venture capital or angel investors may reduce or eliminate personal guarantees, it is more likely that if you own your own business you will be required to give your open-ended personal guarantee over and over again. In the end, if an entrepreneur's business fails, the personal guarantees will be the leading factor in the personal loss.

Unfortunately, there is very little education available about personal guarantees and managing or mitigating them. Here are some ideas, but realize that comprehensive strategies and details would fill a book of their own.

PERSONAL BALANCE SHEETS

The personal guarantee is seen by lenders and others as the way to access the entrepreneur's assets as the "secondary source of repayment" in case of default. Normally banks will require entrepreneurs to prepare a personal balance sheet listing all of their assets and liabilities. There is little to no information regarding what precautions to use in preparing these statements. For example, there is a huge difference between listing assets net of taxes in the case of liquidation versus including taxes. Also, what assets do you list? If you have trusts, do you list the trusts? I spent years in litigation over these matters with Bank of America.

Personal guarantees have a huge impact on the entrepreneur, as you'll see in Mike Brown's tale of tremendous success and loss.

BROWN FAMILY COMMUNITIES

Mike Brown entered his father's home-building business in 1995 as a vice president of operations. Within four years he helped transform the business and effectively doubled its size; more importantly, he developed systems, staffing, and processes that made it operate with predictable and extremely profitable results. Operations were so strong that his father retired to a ranch in Colorado, leaving Mike in charge.

Mike Brown is the former CEO of Brown Family Communities in Phoenix, Arizona. From 1995 until 2005 he grew the family business to $300 million in sales with 350 employees. YPO member.

Soon sales reached about $300 million, and pretax profit was about $34 million. Things were great. That's when his father wanted to take over the business again. He offered to buy back Mike's portion of the business. Mike agreed to a sizable down payment as well as a five-year installment plan. He left the company in 2005, and his father took over operations.

Within months, his father unwound many of Mike's operational processes and policies. Nearly half the staff left. As sales slowed during the initial stages of the real estate crisis, Mike's father made less than ideal decisions, which caused substantial losses. Mike survived but lost about 30 percent of his nest egg when Brown Family Communities shuttered its doors in 2008.

Normally that wouldn't be the end of the world. However, Mike's financial planning involved investments based upon his buy-out installments. And that scenario had changed.

Mike recounted his story: "I had a plan; I sat down and said this is how we can afford to live. My lifestyle was nice. It was beyond nice, and I was living at that level because I could afford it.

"Then one Monday morning in '08, I got a curveball thrown at me. Thirty percent of my estate—all cash—was chopped out. That hurt me so badly that I had to scramble on all the other business deals I had in progress. I had to figure out how to sell those deals and manage them on 30 percent fewer assets and income. As you know, the market was nonexistent, and it wasn't going to get better for years."

The result was that Mike found himself on a virtual treadmill—trying to get out of other business deals at a time when the market was crashing and no one had any idea when it would hit bottom.

Mike continued, "I ended up losing much of my remaining cash on three of the other business deals I was invested in. I had partners, but when things started to go south, they said, 'Well, you've got all the money, why should I pitch in?' I had agreed to be the main guarantor—a mistake I made on a couple of the deals. My partners were also guarantors, but the bank didn't want to chase all of the partners; they decided to chase me. I had to negotiate deals to get me off the personal guarantees."

Mike had three large real estate projects—two in Arizona and one in Utah. His partners more or less bailed on him, leaving Mike responsible for settling with the banks.

"I had a 40,000-square-foot office building with five hangers," Mike said, "and when it was full, it was great. Then the recession hit, and vacancies skyrocketed. My partner came to me and said, 'Hey, I can't help shore up the shortfall.' Who made up the $50,000 a month shortfall? I did.

"I could've gotten out of all of it, if I hadn't been thrown a curveball and lost 30 percent of my cash. That started a domino effect. Diligently, I started selling everything and negotiating with creditors. I sank a lot of my remaining capital in settling with the banks, and they took what they could get from me.

"There are different asset classes, such as single-family residences, multi-family residences, office buildings, and raw land. I'd never again sign a guarantee for a non-revenue-generating asset, such as raw land. I just wouldn't do it.

"I've now settled all of it and think I did the right thing."

Mike paid out about $9.5 million of his nest egg—after-tax dollars from his personal funds—to settle his accounts.

A PREDATORY LENDER

Mike went on, "It took about a year to settle with the banks. I'm not going to mention the lender, one of the most unscrupulous, disgusting bunch of predatory lenders. I went to the banker and asked for an opportunity to pay the debt, but the banker said, 'No, we want the asset.' One of the owners of the bank wanted to park his jet in one of our new hangers. The owner of the bank wanted my building!

"If you want to touch on lessons learned, I can tell you this—it was a humbling experience. I just took the little things in my life for granted when we were riding high. I can tell you they don't mean the same thing to me today. The things that didn't cost anything, I missed the most—things like spending time with my kids. Instead, I cherished a car that I would give to my kids. I look back and realize how fortunate I was—I *still* am fortunate. Once you know how to be successful, nobody can take that away from you. If you drop me ten stories, I'll land on my feet; I'll dust myself off and start over again. I'm going to scrape and claw. I've got the skill set."

AN OCCASIONAL EXCEPTION

Occasionally, you will find a lender who is kinder and gentler, one who doesn't grind the entrepreneur to the bone trying to collect every last cent owed. One of the entrepreneurs profiled in Chapter 9, Brad Adams, had his long-standing wire-stamping and injection molding business forced into bankruptcy. However, Brad had a magnificent experience with his senior lender, who released him from his $5 million personal guarantee because of the way he handled his company's challenges and continued with thorough, honest communication.

We've heard it over and over again: Maintain transparent and thorough communication with your lenders.

HARDBALL LENDERS

Mike McKeough is a Michigan-based land developer and CEO of McKeough Land Company. By 2007, when the Great Recession bore down, Mike had about $57 million in accumulated debt with seventeen different lenders. Some of his company's earlier loans included his wife as a personal guarantor. Through tough negotiations, great communication, and lots of hard work, he brought the debt down to about $20 million, and over the years was able to pay off most of the debts, including the loans his wife also guaranteed. Of the seventeen lenders, only three played hardball with him. One even filed fraud charges against him, which was personally very painful for Mike.

Another of the more aggressive lenders was a wealthy individual. Mike recalled one particular encounter: "I saw him in a restaurant in town, and we probably had a $30 bottle of wine, or something like that, on the table. I got a scathing call from him the next day, saying, 'If I ever see you drinking another $30 bottle of wine, I don't care about ever getting my money back. I'm just going to make sure you go down.'

Mike continued, "That was a very personal event. He was the first creditor who really started pushing. He was the first to come out swinging with a lawsuit.

"Later a debtor's exam ended up finding a major tax refund that we had personally gotten. We had received about $3 million in tax refunds over an eighteen-month period. We used some of the refund to pay off the bank and to keep the company going, and some of the cash we were trying to save to see what we could salvage. Our legal counsel told us half that money belonged to my wife.

"We had set up our company as an S-corporation; essentially, we made big profits, made distributions to myself as a shareholder, put the refunds in a joint checking account, filed joint tax returns, and paid the taxes jointly. When the tax refunds came, they came to us jointly.

"Deciding who really owned those tax refunds led us into a major legal wrangling. We couldn't find any good legal precedent as to who was entitled to the refunds. It was unclear whether they were half mine and half hers, or if the refunds were all mine because it was ultimately some income I earned, or if they were joint property that neither individual creditor could get."

We'll discuss Mike's story in greater detail in Chapter 12, but in the end, Mike ended up trading most of the cash from the tax refund for an inherited IRA that his bankruptcy trustee had wanted to take from him. However, the fighting added about a year and a half to his bankruptcy.

A HOME BUILDER'S STORY

Richard is a CEO of a large home builder in Southern California. His overall story was covered in Chapter 8; here we examine his personal guarantees.

Richard said, "The community banks took a flyer on me, and they said, 'Look, you know our regulatory requirements, so we have to have personal guarantees, but we'll never chase you.' When the president of a bank tells you that, you tend to take it seriously. Not doing so would be a big mistake.

"If that bank becomes a jeopardized institution, then they kick out the president and all the executive management. Now you've got a new set of people, or the acquiring bank comes in with new people.

"We borrowed from a lot of banks. I fell for the community bankers who said, 'We are the guys who got you started, so keep borrowing from us.' I should have just said no, because larger banks would lend to us without the personal guarantees. With the small banks, I should have made the lack of guarantees a deal point. Instead, I had larger lenders who took just my corporate guarantee. I had about $56 million of corporate entity net value with audited financials."

Richard succeeded in removing his personal guarantee from most of the company's debt; however, he had backed about 40 percent of the debt with his personal guarantees. As a result, Richard spent years liquidating assets and undercutting the market even in tough times to induce people to buy. Even if he was taking 15 to 20 percent losses, he knew the market was falling, and he wanted to liquidate as much as possible to reduce his personal liability and ultimately save his equity.

Richard added, "In these scenarios you have to say to buyers, 'Here is a great deal. I need you to buy this . . . I'm desperate.'

"There are degrees of desperation. You need to sacrifice those bragging rights and really play possum to save your life. Pride is a deterrent for people trying to successfully get through these situations."

BANKS HAVE TO SEE YOUR PAIN

By using these tactics, Richard was ultimately able to pay off the entire 40 percent of the corporate debt that had personal guarantees. However, it was difficult.

He said, "In order for the bank to be willing to absorb the loss, they've got to see you in some pain. We had to clean up our personal balance sheet. You're going to sell the yacht; you've got to sell your Porsche; you've got to sell your airplanes; you've got to sell your toys. You're lucky if you can keep your house. You are negotiating with a midlevel bank manager who lives in a production home, and his kids may or may not go to private school.

"Telling them, 'Hey, I liquidated the yacht. I liquidated the second home. I liquidated the beach house' . . . liquidation isn't enough. They want your lifestyle trimmed down. You want the bankers to say, 'Okay, this guy gets it. He's not trying to live the life, and I'm not going to be made a fool for financing his lifestyle.'

"In addition to that, you have to come to the table with some real pain. I mean, on some of these cases, I had to write $750,000 checks. On a short sale, I wrote a $1 million check, but the bank wrote $7 million. The bankers are not going to take pain if you are not taking pain. They have to look at your balance sheet and see how much pain you've taken. You have to lay it out for them in some fair and justifiable manner, because what you are looking at across the table is a midlevel manager."

RANCON DEVELOPMENT

Dan Stephenson is a highly experienced land developer in California, and we explored his company, Rancon Development, and its experiences with recessions in Chapter 7.

He recounted what happened with his personal guarantees: "I don't know if we can be critical of ourselves. During the Great Recession, we had to last five years through the downturn. I don't care how smart you are, you couldn't anticipate it. I like to think I'm very moral and ethical, and I believe if you sign a guarantee you should pay what you owe. The reason I've played a little bit more hardball with these banks—where I'm not dealing with individual investors—is that I think the banks really screwed us all over, the public as well as corporations. They just lent money so stupidly. Their practices created a fever. If you didn't borrow money, you were a fool."

Dan talked about the relaxation of underwriting standards and the competitive pressures it placed on banks: "Poor banks that had really good standards wanted 20 percent down for creditable borrowers. If they held to their standards, they wouldn't make any loans; therefore, their stock didn't go up. Stockholders put pressure on them, so the next thing you know, they're doing high-leverage Small Business Administration loans and everything else. The entire financial institution industry didn't do right by itself, nor did it do right by the American public. I guess I'm hiding a little bit behind those feelings when I play hardball with the banks, when in reality I've signed the guarantee. I should pay it."

Dan's perspective on the differences between banks is pointed and hard earned: "They're all in business to protect their assets. I have to laugh when people say, 'Boy, I hate Wells Fargo, because they've stiffed me on my loan. I'm going to go to another bank because they're nicer.' I don't like Wells Fargo, and I don't do business with them because they have no conscience about stiffing their borrowers. Yet bankers say their job is to protect the bank's assets. They are the first ones to cut and run during a recession. Yes, that's really their job.

"In reality, there are no loyalties. That realization helps us know that banks are representing their depositors and their stockholders, not you as a borrower. Don't be naïve—don't be mad at any bank because they're doing what they're supposed to do."

THE BANKER'S PERSPECTIVE

Part of the research for this book included interviews with two commercial banking executives, and I asked for their views on personal guarantees.

Gary Votapka, who has more than thirty-five years of banking experience, said, "One of the lessons that you learn in banking is that there are certain things that you do. Banks take the guarantee of the owner of the company with the obvious implicit threat that—if something doesn't go right—you've got to go after that owner. You're going to sue him, and you know you're going to make life miserable for him. As a banker, I figured out quickly that 'how the business goes, so goes the owner.' The owner is much more nimble than the bank could ever be. If he or she hid assets, then, when it finally got to the point that you're going to sue somebody, unless they were really stand-up people, there would be nothing of consequence there.

"Time and time again, when you finished working on the borrower side and you went after the guarantor side, there was little to go after. Why would the bank spend $25,000 in legal expenses to go after a guy when the outcome is usually the same? You know the guy is going to go bankrupt or something else will happen, and you've spent money unnecessarily.

"Because there were a number of times when an owner mistreated the bank or acted wrongly, we bankers want to take it personally. The customer caused you to lose hundreds of thousands of dollars, so you want to make your statement to them.

"However, as a banker and as a businessperson, you've got to get over that feeling and make a good business decision. Suing the individual should only be done with the obvious strategy of having a positive financial impact and an outcome that's favorable to the bank, or you don't do it."

LESSONS LEARNED

- Eliminate or reduce the scope of any personal guarantees for loans, sureties, and so on.

- Talk to prospective banks on workout policies, personal guarantees, and the like.

- Banks are in the business to protect their assets, not yours.

- If you're negotiating a settlement, especially if you are close to being illiquid, playing possum may be very effective.

- Focus on eliminating liabilities with personal guarantees as your priority.

- If you are negotiating settlements, reduce your lifestyle and show the bankers your pain.

CHAPTER 12

YOUR BANKER IS NOT YOUR FRIEND

*"If you want to be in business in the future,
you're going to need the banks in later years."*

anks can be your biggest friend or your worst enemy. The irony is
that the same bank can fill both roles. Of course, there is a huge
spectrum of banks, and they each have different approaches and
philosophies. I recommend that you interview the folks at your banking
institution and find out what some of their approaches are, which
groups handle problem loans, their attitude toward enforcing personal
guarantees, and so on. Ask other entrepreneurs about their experiences
with banks in good times and, perhaps more critically, in bad times.

This chapter reviews the challenges and experiences that entrepreneurs have had with banks, providing insight on how they have been
treated by those institutions and how they've responded in return.

When the banking relationship is new and times are good, you
will be dealing with nice professional people. These are effectively the
sales representatives for the bank. However, generally speaking, when
covenants are broken and difficulties arise in the business, responsibility

for the loan is transferred to the "workout group." This is a totally different and, for the most part, ruthless team, who in no way resemble the bankers who created the relationship in the first place. The workout group is often located in a separate building, maybe even in a different region. They usually have little interaction with, or resemblance to, your good-guy bankers. The experiences of some of the entrepreneurs we've discussed bear this out.

Bob Verdun, the Detroit-based software company founder, learned that his bank had such tight restrictions on his company's cash that he wouldn't know until five p.m. on paydays whether his employees' payroll checks would clear. His bank clamped down so hard on him and his firm that he found it difficult to manage the company; the bank seriously amplified his problems. Of course, that level of stress on the organization caused employees to leave.

Jim Glazer, the Nebraska-based specialty-truck manufacturer, noted that for years his company was allowed to increase debt to the point that there was little to no profit left in the company. He almost lost his business in 2011 but eventually turned things around. He added, "I now realize that debt is not infinite and that the bankers are not your friends."

AMERICAN MOLDING

Matt Hagen is a brilliant man who graduated from USC, worked at Arthur Anderson in its mergers and acquisitions division, and by 2001 had completed his MBA from Harvard. That's when he joined his father's company, American Molding, which manufactured and distributed building products to Home Depot and others. The company had grown to sales in excess of $100 million but was now losing money. Matt headed distribution in Washington, DC, and by 2003, he had become the president of that division.

Matt Hagen graduated from USC and later earned a Harvard MBA. As president of his family-owned company, American Molding, a manufacturer and distributor of building products, he grew it to $220 million in 2007. YPO member.

Matt recalled the course of events; "When I became president of the business, it was right at the beginning of that huge growth period for the housing-products industry. I spent the better part of the first four years as an absolute hero. Everything that I did worked. Money was cheap. I bought a number of companies, all with debt. We took a lot of cash out of the business and distributed it to do various things; the business had a lot of debt but was also making lots and lots of money.

"From 2001 to 2005, the company went from losing money to being incredibly profitable, resulting in a healthy balance sheet; it was worth a lot of money. Unbeknownst to me, however, at that time just about everybody in the building-products space was making lots of money. I just thought I was brilliant.

"In 2007, I had just finished buying another company, and I had not yet known any adversity in the business. Our culture was to keep things close to the chest with a very tight group of people. There wasn't a lot of transparency for our management team, and there was very little transparency for our bankers, other than the good stuff we wanted to share. That was just our M.O. We didn't want to share much with anybody because the information was incredibly personal to the family."

LEVERAGING UP

Matt continued, "We acquired another business in '07, again with all debt, and we leveraged up some more. Just after closing, the legs came out from underneath the building-products industry. We had used so much cash predominantly to grow and invest in expansion of our base outside of Home Depot, that we tapped massive amounts of profitability.

Instead of paying down debt, we used the cash to grow and diversify. There was no liquidity in the business when things got soft.

"That was 2007, and Bank of America was our lender. Bank of America had a mandate to get out of the building-products industry. So Bank of America was brutal, and Wachovia and PNC were also in on the deal. I didn't share the true distress of the business with our employees and certainly not with our bank.

"Ultimately, Bank of America said, 'You need to go raise money.' I hired an investment bank they had recommended. This was the climax of me being green and untested from both a communication standpoint and not understanding how these bank workout guys operated. I said to my family, 'Here's an investment advisor who was recommended to me; he also has restructuring experience that can help me raise some money in this distressed climate.' This was just a pipe dream, but I didn't know it at the time. I hired them, and of course Bank of America and Wachovia approved them."

INVESTMENT BANKER OR RESTRUCTURING ADVISOR?

"Our management had a call on a Tuesday with the investment banking advisor," said Matt. "By the end of the call, he had transformed the relationship into that of a restructuring advisor. Later, we learned that people behind the scenes at Wachovia and this restructuring group had predetermined the outcome.

"The restructuring advisor was deeply involved for the better part of six months, charging $200,000 a month. He absolutely trashed the Hagen family's reputation to our employees, to our trade creditors, and to the people that mattered most, Home Depot. He talked about everything that we did wrong and how we were unethical—all in an effort to entrench his firm into the business and to put it in a position to act as an investment banking advisor, sell the business, and get another fee. He and his group ignored any sort of ethics that come with representing the business they should protect. Their action was clearly about covering their own asses and extracting as much value as they could; in the process, they tried to destroy our reputation.

"Within thirty days of hiring the firm, I had essentially been fired from my family business and told not to come back. The restructuring advisor basically told me, 'The bank doesn't welcome your presence here. You're not trusted. In order for us to execute this plan, we need you to step away. We'll call you when we need you.'

"And when I look back on it, I think, how could I possibly have let that happen? It was just a mindblower to me how I let those things come to pass. It was a crisis. The bank was threatening liquidation. We were in default, and they could force us into Chapter 11. They kept that hammer on us. One of my worst moments was walking out of there, fired from my own company but still trying to preserve the lending relationship to keep the business going.

"From an operational perspective, they actually did a decent job on the restructuring side. Most of the playbook they executed was the stuff we had teed up and had ready to go. They just continued with the plan.

"Ultimately, I hired an alternative firm to be an investment banking advisor, to take that area of responsibility away from the restructuring group. Then I went to my attorney—which I should have done earlier—and talked to him about what was going on. Essentially, I threatened a lender-liability lawsuit."

LENDER LIABILITY

Matt said, "They were not acting as a restructuring advisor; instead, they were behaving as the CEO of the business. To a certain degree, they were acting at the direction of the bank, which falls squarely in the realm of lender liability. I notified them in writing about the role they were playing, explaining that 'they had exceeded their authority beyond acting as an advisor to the Hagens and that they had really been acting in the interest of themselves and the bank.' I got a lot out of the threat of a lender-liability lawsuit. Many of the things that were going on came to a screeching halt.

"I was able to get my CFO put in as president, with authority to conduct business. The restructuring guys backed off in a major way and began to act the way they should have from the beginning, which was as advisors, not as officers of the company.

"We were able to get a term sheet from United Commercial Bank out of San Francisco to refinance Bank of America. To do that, we sold many of our personal assets, leveraged a residence that had a high appraisal, and borrowed by putting a corporate guarantee against it. Basically, we leveraged everything we had. The day we closed I left the office and opened a bottle of champagne. It was one of the single most important moments of my entire life."

Matt and his family had tumbled into the abyss and survived.

MCKEOUGH LAND COMPANY

Western Michigan native Mike McKeough graduated from Lake Forest College in Illinois. In 1989, just a couple years after graduation, he started McKeough Land Company. It took until 2000 for his land sales company to break $1 million, but soon after that the firm began serious growth.

Mike McKeough is from Western Michigan. In 1989, just a couple years after graduating from Lake Forest College, he started McKeough Land Company and grew it to about $37 million in sales. Later he started Terra Firma Management. YPO member.

Mike discussed what happened to his company: "Very quickly between 2002 and 2005, we grew the business to about $37 million in sales. We were selling lots in seven or eight states; we had five regional offices with a good management team in place, and we were cranking.

"We were good at what we were doing, but I think a lot of the growth was because we were in an industry that was riding a tidal wave of real estate investment, and people were spending beyond their means. We rode that wave up, and we were quite profitable in the process. We always averaged somewhere between a 20 and 30 percent net-profit margin. As you can imagine with a high-growth company, we reinvested most of that money back into the business.

"We didn't have a lot of outside personal wealth, but in 2004 we built a nice home into which I put about a million dollars of personal cash. I continued to grow the business, and then, in 2006, things started to slow. I should have seen the writing on the wall earlier than I did.

"We used to do marketing campaigns and spend maybe $100,000 on a big-project grand opening. We would get a couple of thousand prospects. In 2006, we had similar numbers, but our marketing budget was more than twice as much to get the same number of prospects.

"We were still quite profitable, so that didn't concern us terribly. By early 2007, however, the wheels started falling off; our sales just plummeted. We had sales of about $12 million, but we had $53 million in debt at the time, so we were barely covering our overhead. When we added in our debt load, we were underwater.

"We reacted quickly. I brought in a friend of mine, a former CEO with turnaround experience. He quickly came up with a plan to take to our banks. We got them to decrease the amount we had to pay when we sold any lots that were security for one of their loans. We also got them to kick in another $2 million of operating capital, which was quite an accomplishment. Eight of our thirteen lenders agreed to kick in more cash, based on how much money they had already loaned to us. The $2 million was to help try to keep us afloat.

"We did almost daily reporting, and we had to get all of our extensions approved. For a little while it looked like the plan might work; however, after a year we were sort of floundering. We didn't need to borrow any additional money, but we weren't able to improve our balance sheet.

"Eventually, a couple of banks pulled out, and then it was every bank for itself. Some of the banks started coming after us in various ways, but we were able to negotiate settlements with most of them."

TERRA FIRMA MANAGEMENT

"We started a new company called Terra Firma Management," Mike continued. "At the time, McKeough Land Company was about nineteen years old. Essentially, we shut its doors, because we knew McKeough was too far underwater to try to do anything with. We deeded all our properties to the banks that were working with us. The banks then hired Terra Firma Management to market and sell the properties for them. They paid us a decent fee, which allowed us to keep thirty-five or forty of our employees as our key group. At the same time, some of the other banks were coming after us. Their actions were mostly friendly foreclosing stuff, just to clean things up.

"There was one bank where I had been on the board of directors. The president and a couple of the key officers of this branch had left the bank, so our loan file went up to the corporate offices. It was a complex loan, and they didn't really understand it. They decided that something must be amiss, so they sued us for fraud.

"Eight years of my life on the board of this bank were for nothing. I had been a big fan of that community bank and thought serving on their board of directors was the right thing to do, but they turned on me. We fought that lawsuit tooth and nail, and finally the court threw it out; however, it was a very stressful situation."

SETTLEMENTS AND BANKRUPTCY

"Ultimately," Mike said, "Terra Firma Management worked itself out of a job. We sold through a lot of the inventory for the banks and recovered a lot of their money. The average bank that worked with us probably lost about half of its loan principal. The banks that didn't work with us lost three quarters of their money. When we did a deed in lieu of foreclosure to the banks, in about 70 percent of the cases they released us from any personal liability. By 2009 my $57 million of debt was reduced to about $20 million. There were more deals that I could have done, but by 2010 I had to file personal bankruptcy.

"By that time Terra Firma had morphed into a management company and was no longer working on bank projects. We purchased one project back from a bank, a nice northern Michigan ski and golf resort development. We also bought inexpensive distressed properties in my area."

In 2009, in the midst of Mike's financial headaches, his son was involved in a horrific boating accident that killed the son's best friend and cost another friend her leg. The accident was devastating for the family and the community, and for years afterward, Mike and his wife were concerned for their son's emotional safety. He is now doing well and thriving, but the accident prompted additional legal challenges that lasted many years.

Nevertheless Mike retained a well-balanced attitude about his challenges: "Maybe a difference between me and others is that many people who are in my situation blame the banks; I think that's the most ridiculous thing in the world."

Understanding his responsibility for the situation helped Mike land back on his feet.

COMPARTMENTALIZING

Richard, the anonymous CEO of the home-building company in Southern California worked like mad to get off the hook of his corporate and personal debt. He discussed working with the banks while keeping the end game in mind:

"You need to compartmentalize as much as you can. If you want to be in business in the future, you're going to need the banks later. You have to negotiate with that future relationship in mind. You have to think, 'I want your bank to be there for me when I get started again.'

"So I looked at the banking relationships, and I compartmentalized. I told myself *these* are people that I can do business with again, whereas Bank of America . . . I won't. I knew they were bad guys from before. After the early '90s recession, they had come back and said, 'We are the new kinder, gentler bank.' Nah, that's BS.

"You compartmentalize and utilize your remaining assets to preserve the future business relationship. You've got to have the end in mind. I need certain lenders to say, 'That was a bad situation, but he handled it in a stand-up fashion.' I got lucky. I have fourteen lenders, and thirteen of them will say that about me."

Richard's approach was highly effective, compared to others in that industry who chose to fight through a multitude of lawsuits. If you sit down with each lender and methodically devise a plan, you're far better off.

LESSONS LEARNED

- Before establishing a banking relationship, interview the bankers. Find out how they handle workouts. Ask about their enforcement of personal guarantees.

- Borrow conservatively. There are cycles where debt is cheap and readily available. Use debt without overleveraging your business.

- Ask to be removed from personal guarantees often and early. If you can't have them removed, limit them. Have "carve-outs" for guarantees that exempt your home and certain other assets.

- Personal guarantees for debt or other liabilities should not exceed the amount of the debt you are guaranteeing. Do not enter into an unlimited, open guarantee.

CHAPTER 13

ACQUISITIONS, LEVERAGE, AND BANKS

"Buying a company for money—anybody can do that.
But buying a company for nothing—that's art."

A cquisitions and roll-up strategies can be very risky. I've always said that about 80 percent of acquisitions either fail completely or, at a minimum, fail to meet the expected returns. It's important to understand that and be ready; hopefully you will increase your scrutiny of any deal before pulling the trigger on an acquisition. Growth through acquisition and the use of debt for growth are the subjects of this chapter.

Alejandro Rivas Micoud, the Spanish entrepreneur mentioned in Chapter 4, told me a story that illustrated how quirky some deals can be: "In early 2000 I was desperately trying to find some kind of solution to our company's finances. I had lunch with a well-known person in Spain who had a shady reputation. I was asking if he was willing to invest in the company. At a certain point he said, 'You know what? Buying a company for money—anybody can do that. But buying a company for nothing—that's art.' I thought he was full of BS at the time, but I found out that he was right. It can be done, though, of course, a lot depends on being at the right place at the right time."

GLOBAL PACK

Scott Dickman is a fast-moving entrepreneur. He graduated with a law degree in the 1980s and became a corporate counsel and securities attorney. He didn't want to spend his career charging by the hour, however, and wanted to do more for his family. After he received a nice payout from taking a client company public on the London Stock Exchange, he decided to look for a company to purchase.

Scott Dickman graduated from the University of Tulsa with a law degree and became a successful securities lawyer. After buying several food-packaging plants, he grew Pinnacle Packaging to about $250 million in sales with 800 employees. YPO member.

He discussed becoming an entrepreneur: "In 2000 I started talking to friends in investment banking and really zeroed in on the packaging industry. I liked the consistency, and I felt like it was sustainable through the evolutions of the economy. I found this small mom-and-pop company in Toledo, Ohio, that made butter cartons. If the carton didn't have Land o' Lakes' name on it, this company made the butter carton. The business was very automated; it ran 24/7. There wasn't a lot of margin, but it was a very steady, easy business. It was something I felt I could get my head around. I acquired it, and in our first year we did about $2.5 million in sales.

"We were able to expand that company pretty well. Then about a year and a half later, International Paper decided to sell two of its facilities, and we were in the mix to look at them. We ended up buying only one of the companies, located in Georgia. It made all the Krispy Kreme doughnut boxes, JC Penny boxes, and a lot of folding cartons.

We thought it was a good add-on to what we were doing. We were excited and did really well with it. We were able to expand the business, and we got some great people out of that acquisition, allowing us to raise our game a little bit.

"Then in 2003, we got a call from International Paper. They said, 'We really want to show you this plant in North Carolina, because it's the sister plant to the one you bought.' However, it was a big, big plant. I mean it was doing $30 or $40 million a year in sales. I just didn't think I could take that on. They said, 'No, no, no, we'll help you buy this. We *want* you to buy this. We don't want to put this out in the market.'

"The factory made folding cartons for Pepsi and the thirty-six-packs of cans for Sam's Club and Walmart. They also made the paper baskets for Smirnoff Ice and Coors, and things like that. It was a nice plant with really good people. Within a few years, we'd put all three of these companies together, and we were really doing well; we got up to about $80 million in sales. We completed that deal in 2003, and we really felt good about where we were.

"Around that same time, R. J. Reynolds Tobacco Company (RJR) had decided they were going to sell their packaging group. We thought there was no way we could even be a player, but we wanted to put our name in the mix. The plant was really big. However, RJR was also in North Carolina, so it wasn't very far from our other plant. We got to know the guys at the RJR plant, and we worked with them for two years on that.

"RJR put their plant out for bid, and we were the winner. Then they took it back off the market, because they did a merger with another tobacco company and decided to wait on the sale of the packaging company. After the merger, they decided to put it back on the market; the problem was that they didn't want to sell their company to someone who was just going to turn around and sell them packaging. They wanted a buyer who was going to build a large plant just for them. That was a $100 million dollar investment, so there was no way we were going to do that.

"However, in 2005, we agreed to buy their packaging group and provide their packaging until the new company could build their facilities and start providing their packaging needs. It was a big investment for us, and very exciting, because what we really wanted was the flexible packaging, the non-tobacco stuff. By the end of that acquisition, we were doing flexible packaging, which is where we felt we'd get the highest margins. We were producing the foil lids for Yoplait Yogurt and pouches for Tylenol. When we acquired the RJR contract, we had about 800 employees. All combined, we did about $250 million in sales with about $18 to $19 million in EBITDA in 2006.

"We were growing exponentially; it was a mushroom story!"

AN UNFORESEEN DISASTER

Scott continued, "One of our plants in North Carolina was an aluminum-casting mill, where we made our own aluminum foil, which made us unique in the industry. On February 19, 2007, that plant had a fire and explosion. It was devastating, absolutely devastating. Fortunately, nobody got hurt. We had our own fire brigades, and they were fantastic. I'm convinced to this day that they saved people's lives, and we had an angel on our shoulders. Not one person had a scratch.

"But the building was gone—it was obliterated. When I got there that day, the fire department captain told me that they thought it would be a recovery mission, since there was no way that people could have gotten out of there alive. But they did head counts, and not one person was hurt. We were amazed.

"We had really good insurance, but it took us nine months to rebuild. Right before that, I had consolidated all of our corporate debt into one bank, instead of having each plant with its own credit facility. I thought I was smart. When we had the fire, I called Wells Fargo, and they said, 'Well, your loan officer doesn't work here anymore. We'll have your new loan officer call you.'

"Someone I had never talked to and never heard of called me, and I told him the story. He said, 'Oh, my gosh! Well, this is a lot. I'm going to have to talk to somebody who specializes in this stuff and call you back.' I got a call from the workout guy in Houston, and he was pretty gruff.

"I'm being nice here. He was really not a good guy. He came to the plant, and we could not get him out of the conference room. He had no interest in seeing the plant, meeting the people, or doing anything. All he wanted was the loan paid off. He wanted us to move it. I told him there was no way I could move our loan until I got the insurance taken care of and until we got the plant rebuilt and were back on our feet. His response was, 'Nope, that's not it. We are going to confiscate all the insurance proceeds.'

"Fortunately, I had separated the real estate into a private company. I held the real estate myself and leased it back to the company. This provided some personal assets that I could trade or sell to make the bank more comfortable. I transferred the real estate from me to the company in exchange for the bank's leaving me alone so I could restructure the debt. To do that, I had to sell two of our plants. I was reluctant, but I felt like it was necessary to save the bigger company."

SELLING OFF

"Selling the two plants pared down the packaging company quite a bit," said Scott. "Our revenue was down to about $125 million. We were doing pretty well, making more than $10 million in EBITDA, but we knew we could still be doing better. We had to make some investments in our equipment and drop that aluminum-casting site, because it was very capital intensive.

"About this time, we started doing the Tropicana juice cartons. Tropicana became $25 million of our $125 million in sales. We were their second supplier. We did 300 million of those cartons a year and were very good at it.

"However, by 2009 we decided to sell the company. We got a great offer of $63 million, and since we didn't have a lot of debt on it, we accepted the offer.

"It was a good private equity firm, and two months after the letter of intent (LOI) was signed, Tropicana decided to switch to plastic. We knew we were going to lose some of that business. We went to the private equity firm and explained; I wanted to be very upfront and honest. They said, 'Okay, we appreciate it, but let's just wait and see what happens in six months or so when things normalize after the Tropicana deals are over.' We did that.

"You know, we definitely were a smaller company. By that time, our sales were $100 million, and we were doing about $8 million in EBITDA. They said, 'We'd still like to do it, however, we are thinking now the company is only worth about $40 million.' We needed another six months or so to prove to them that we were going to be fine; then we would get a higher valuation.

"Later, we got a call from another private equity firm called Centre Lane Partners. I didn't know it at the time, but it used to be part of the private equity firm that made us the first offer."

CENTRE LANE PARTNERS

Scott continued, "Centre Lane was also buying a company called LL Flex, which was one of our customers; we were selling them aluminum. Centre Lane's intent was to buy us and merge us with LL Flex to have a good platform. I thought that was a good idea and said that we would entertain it, and they gave us a LOI for $53 million, which we signed. All of a sudden, LL Flex started canceling orders, but we'd already made the foil. They just stopped taking it. They were playing inventory games, because their closing with the private equity firm was set for December 31, and working capital was a factor in the purchase price.

"If LL Flex took the inventory, that would increase their inventory numbers, lowering the sales price. Therefore, they started delaying orders. That wreaked havoc with us, because we didn't have enough credit line, and we were stuck with about $2 million of inventory. That had never happened to us before. We had sold to LL Flex for years and years. We had to furlough people. It was a terrible time.

"Centre Lane used that to their advantage and came back and renegotiated the price. We weren't happy about it, but at this point Wells Fargo was not being very cooperative; the bank was getting antsy. We entered into an LOI with Centre Lane on March 19, 2012. Then one day they called me and said, 'Look, we don't think we want the aluminum mill. We only want the flexible packaging group. Do you have any interest in keeping the mill, or do you know somebody that would?'

"I said that I might: 'I'd be happy to look around and talk to people about it, and I'll get back to you. But I want you to continue doing your due diligence, because I have to get this closed before our loan renews on May 31.'

"I started talking to some people," said Scott, "but at the same time I didn't really trust these guys. There was just something about them that wasn't right. I didn't feel that they really had the money to close on time, so I also began talking to some banks about refinancing. I talked to PNC and Bank of America, and we got proposals and term sheets from both of them. Somehow, word of that got out from our people. Centre Lane sent letters to all the people I was talking to about the mill, as well as to these banks, saying that we'd signed an LOI and they had no right to talk to us—that they were interfering in the Centre Lane contract.

"The lawyers start getting involved, and I wrote a letter to them. Of course, May 30 came around, but Centre Lane was not in a position to close; they'd filed suit against me in Delaware. They claimed that I'd violated the exclusivity provision of the LOI. We countersued them for tortuous interference, and although the bankers were not amused, they gave us an extension to July 6.

"Then they asked me to appoint a Chief Restructuring Officer (CRO). I thought, 'Oh, what the hell, I don't really care. I'm going to keep plodding along until I refinance. If that's what I have to do for the bank, that's what I have to do.'

"These CRO guys don't come cheap. You pay them $250,000, plus you're paying the bank $150,000 each time you get an amendment to the loan agreement. We paid almost $2 million in fees between December and August 10, when this whole thing ended.

"By July 3, I had tried to talk with the banks as well as another private equity firm. Everybody said, 'You're in litigation. We would love to do a loan for you, but Centre Lane is very litigious, and there's already a suit going on. We just don't want to get caught in it.'"

ENTER BANKRUPTCY COUNSEL

Scott went on, "At that point I started talking to Chapter 11 counsel. On July 3 I got a call from the Centre Lane guys, saying, 'We want to come to Tulsa to talk to you and see if we can resolve this without going to court.'

"I said, 'Look, guys, I'm going into bankruptcy on July 6.' I knew if we went into bankruptcy here in Oklahoma, the lawsuit they filed in Delaware would get pulled to here, and they would get killed because of the tortuous interference. The Tulsa bankruptcy court would not look kindly at that and would hold them responsible for the difference in purchase price for whatever we received and what they'd offered.

"We entered into a deal with Centre Lane to close by July 31. Because Wells Fargo didn't believe them, it made Centre Lane put some money up front to participate in the loan. Centre Lane invested $750,000 to participate in the loan with Wells on the last-out basis. In other words, Wells had seniority rights, and it was senior to any sub debt.

"In the meantime, I got a call from One Equity Partners (part of JP Morgan) and Constantia Packaging. Constantia, which is owned by One

Equity, is the gold standard, with a lot of experience in the packaging industry. They do what we do, except they do it globally, and we thought that they would be a great fit. However, I just didn't think there was enough time to do the deal.

"I explained the entire situation to Constantia and gave them copies of our agreement and everything else. I told them I didn't think they could close fast enough, but they convinced me they could. They flew their people in, and we discussed all the details.

"Then they said, 'Our concern is Centre Lane. We want to do a deal with you but we want you to negotiate the deal with Centre Lane to make them go away.'

"I said, 'But you guys realize we don't think we really did anything wrong. We think *they* did wrong; we think they owe us a lot of money for the difference in value.'

"One Equity said, 'We will authorize up to $6 million dollars to pay the Centre Lane guys to go away.'

"I said, 'They probably have $1.5 million in it with all the lawyers and everything else. There's no way it's going to cost me that.'

"One Equity said, 'We will let you keep half of whatever the difference is. So if you settle for $2 million you can keep half of the $4 million balance.'

"I said, 'Well, okay, I'll tell you what, I'll go negotiate with Centre Lane.'"

THE PAYOFF

"I talked to Centre Lane," continued Scott, "and said, 'Look, I don't really want to go forward with you guys at this point, but I feel like you guys have some expenses and I want it to be amicable. So I'd rather settle all claims and have you go away.'

"Our exclusivity provision with Centre Lane excluded financing, so we got a letter from them as well that said that we could talk to people about refinancing the deal. We just couldn't talk to people about selling the company. So our discussion with One Equity was about loaning us money to take Wells Fargo completely out if we got Centre Lane to go away. Then, after we got rid of Wells and Centre Lane, Constantia would be interested in a first right of refusal to buy the company.

"When we went to Centre Lane to renegotiate the deal, they found out that a private equity firm was backing me. The price went up from $1.5 million to $1.7 million to $2.3 million, and we settled on $3 million. So we paid them $3 million dollars, and they went away. We signed releases, and we settled the Delaware lawsuit."

A BIG-DOG PHONE CALL

"I was getting antsy," Scott remembered, "and I said to the One Equity guys, 'You don't understand, we've got to get this done.' The head of the One Equity European office called Wells Fargo up the day before the loan was due and said, 'We are One Equity, and we are part of JP Morgan; we're buying this company called Global Pack to bring it into Constantia. We've also got another transaction we are doing.' He kind of 'big-dogged' it. He said, 'This is what we really want to do; we're just looking for forty-five days to do a little more due diligence on this, and so we would like to give you $1 million dollars to stand down for forty-five days.' Basically, they offered to pay Wells a $1 million forbearance fee.

"The One Equity guy continued, 'We'd also give you the opportunity to participate in the loan to buy Global Pack for Constantia, and you'll get a mergers and acquisition fee on this other transaction.' Of course, we weren't on the phone; they wanted to talk banker to banker. We didn't know anything about the call, and we had no knowledge that they were going to talk about that. We had told them all along that Wells had to be paid off. We sent them the payoff letters we had signed with Wells. We had no idea they were going to do anything other than arrange a wire. They were going to be our new lender for the $18 to $20 million Wells Fargo loan.

"So the Wells banker threw a hissy fit and called me. He said, 'You guys told us we were going to get paid off, but we are not going to get paid off.'

"I said, 'I'm completely surprised, I didn't know.'

"Finally, Constantia said, 'Look, we'll front you the working capital you need for the next forty-five days, and if Wells will just draw the cash receipt paying down the loan in addition to standing still, then maybe we can negotiate something.' It just got so convoluted that it wasn't going to work unless One Equity Partners did the deal and paid off the loan."

"MAYBE THAT'S THE BEST THING"

Scott went on, "On August 3 One Equity called me and said, 'Look, we don't think we are going to pursue this any further. We think that with the due diligence that we've done, maybe the company's not going to be worth quite as much as we thought, so we are going to walk away.'

"I said, 'You guys can't just walk away. I put $3 million more debt on this company to make these people go away. You are leaving me with nothing to do but file bankruptcy.'

"They said, 'Well, maybe that's the best thing for you.'

"Now, some of my best friends, family, and YPO forum members were in this deal, but they were never preferred shareholders, so I was devastated. At that point, I just didn't know what else I could do. We started down the road with bankruptcy, and sure enough, Wells called Centre Lane and said, 'Why don't you come back into the deal?'

"Centre Lane came back in and basically bought the deal for the debt. It wiped out at least $20 million of value for me and my family.

"I had thought for a year I would be out by the end of May at the latest, but the deal just kept going on and on. I'm convinced that from the time Centre Lane gave us the first LOI in the fall of 2011, their activities—manipulating the LL Flex inventory and everything else—were designed to make us weaker at each step. As it turned out, Wells Fargo financed Centre Lane to buy the company. We were obviously devastated.

"But, honestly, there was nothing I could do. I couldn't react fast enough. There was nobody I could call up in YPO and say, 'Hey, how do I fix this?' Short of calling Jamie Dimon at JP Morgan, there was nothing I could do. I was screwed, and I didn't see it coming.

"It never occurred to me that One Equity and Constantia would do what they did. They were the gold standard to me. They were the people you would want to align yourself with—the best in the industry. I was devastated from a personal standpoint as well. My family was obviously very upset, and they were worried about me."

LESSONS LEARNED

- Don't get involved in private equity transactions with firms that have unknown or negative reputations.

- Don't allow private equity firms to have exclusivity. More reputable firms will not require exclusivity. If you do agree to it, negotiate all the other details up front.

CHAPTER 14

THE BANKERS' VIEWPOINT

"There was no way to know where the economy
was heading and how bad it was going to get."

B ankers' perspectives are very different from those of business owners, and this chapter shares some insights on lending issues, relationships with entrepreneurs, and the impact of the Great Recession.

I believe bankers' views also vary vastly depending upon the philosophy of the institutional leaders. The entrepreneurs in these pages and I have shared our experiences with Bank of America, Wells Fargo, Morgan Stanley, Wachovia, Comerica, PNC, and others, and I thought it was important to hear from the other side.

MISSION OAKS COMMUNITY BANK

Banker Gary Votapka has been mentioned previously. He is the founder and former CEO of Mission Oaks Bank in Southern California. Gary has an interesting background with thirty-five years of experience: He spent the early part of his career working as an FDIC examiner, looking at financial institutions from the outside and evaluating their data and financial information. Later, with increased responsibilities, he joined a series of banks, gaining significant depth and breadth in his work. However, he had never been a CEO. Around 1998, various friends and acquaintances suggested that he should start and lead a new community bank, and that's what he did.

Gary Votapka earned a BS from Montana State University and started his career as an FDIC examiner. He became founder and CEO of California's Mission Oaks Bank, which was twice ranked in the Top 100 Community Banks.

Gary opened a door into the banker's world and the impact of the Great Recession: "Because of my background and the regulatory process, I felt like I knew how to get the bank formed without the expense of several consultants. I did the administration, and over the next nine months or so, I filed all the paperwork. I jumped through all the hoops, raised the capital, and the regulators approved our charter.

"We opened the bank in the fall of 2000 as a single-office local bank in Temecula. For the next three years, I had to build critical mass in order for the company to be profitable. We were able to execute it well and were right on schedule. We attained profitability and then continued to grow the bank. Economically, that was a good time here in California, and we enjoyed it; the bank really prospered. By 2007 analysts named us among the top 200 community banks in the United States. I think we came in around ninetieth in the nation. Everything was going really well."

THE GREAT RECESSION HITS

"We were up to $250 million in assets," Gary said. "We had five offices and somewhere north of 120 employees. Then the recession hit. I could feel the turn in 2008, but it hit with a vengeance in 2009. About halfway through the end of that year was when it really, really felt like the world was coming to an end. It hit Southern California hard, particularly the Inland Empire, where we were located.

"Unemployment spiked up over 16 percent, with record numbers of foreclosures. At one point, analysts estimated that more than 40 percent of the homes in the Inland Empire were underwater in value. Residential real estate values dropped 40 percent, and raw land dropped 75 to 90 percent.

"As a bank, when you go out to make a loan, you use underwriting criteria. Say we will be asking for a loan of no more than 75 percent on commercial real estate, 80 percent on residential real estate, and 50 percent on land—that kind of thing. When you have drops in value like those that we experienced, it doesn't matter what loan you have. Almost every single loan that had originated in the past ten years was underwater.

"On top of that, there were businesses falling by the wayside right and left. It was just an awful time, and we were scrambling. We were under a lot of pressure from the regulators. I understood that process, and we tried to do what we could, but being in the middle of it, there was no way to know where the economy was heading and how bad it was going to get.

"During that time, there were probably four or five competing community banks in our area that failed. It seemed inevitable that we could fail, too. As a CEO of a company in a situation like that, you have to be able to adjust and set aside your mind-set of, 'I am running a company to prosper, to grow, and to take advantage of business opportunities.' Instead, it becomes, 'I'm fighting for survival at this point. I'm trying to figure what my company has to do in order to get through this.'

"You're closing offices, you're laying employees off, which is just awful to go through. You're sitting down with many of the customers who were your friends and people you've done business with for a long time, having really tough conversations. Sometimes people you thought would never let you down turn on you and do what they have to do. You can't help but feel betrayed. You thought that they would have more respect and consideration for your situation.

"Many people had misrepresented their financial status to the point that it bordered on outright fraud and lies. Some customers had figured out a way to ask you to give them more money than they should have expected.

"Banking is built on trust to a large degree. You have customers who do business with you even though they could go to any large bank. You want to hold on to your good customers, but trying to figure out who they are is an incredible challenge."

REGULATORS

Gary continued, "The regulators do what they have to do in order to clean up the whole banking thing. They don't have the inclination to consider an individual bank's situation; for the most part, they start assuming your bank is like every other bank out there and this is what they're doing to all banks. The tide sweeps all the banks along.

"There were a lot of good banks. Maybe they just happened to have the wrong borrowers, or maybe they were slightly more aggressive or whatever, but they didn't make it.

"We were able to get through the recession. Early on, we had to recapitalize the bank—we had to do a bunch of things. The regulators pressured our board constantly to make changes. The thought was that if you changed management, the new guys would do a better job than the old people would. This is not necessarily true. There is no doubt that a guy who knows how to grow a bank may not be a guy who knows how to take care of it in a downturn. Fortunately, my background was such that I had dealt with many bank problems; a downturn was just another banking problem. So I was equipped to handle the recession.

"Finally, in 2011, the regulators gave my board an ultimatum. They said either you get rid of the top gun, or we'll fine you guys with a civil money penalty. They did fine me. They could have fined everybody on the board, but it was only me that they fined with a relatively small $5,000 civil money penalty to drive home their point."

FORCED TO RESIGN

"The bank's board of directors were my friends," said Gary. "We had been in the partnership for eleven years at that point, and most of them thought, 'Forget the regulators.' I knew that eventually I would have to resign, and there was still the possibility of a bankruptcy, so I tried to position the bank in the best way that I could. I went out and recruited my replacement about a year before I left. That was important to me, because I knew a lot of my family's and friends' wealth was tied up in the bank.

"The fact that I lost a job was only one factor. I had personal reasons why I wanted to see the bank regain its position and to move on: Possibly they could get back whatever wealth had been lost in this recession. I was motivated. I found a guy who could step in, and the board agreed.

"When you go through one of these ordeals, there are emotional and spiritual scars, and you've got to give scars time to heal before you feel like life can go on. I've got to keep going."

Although Gary felt that his successor was doing a good job at the time of our interview, the bank was subsequently sold in an unfriendly sale. At one point he'd been the largest shareholder of Mission Oaks, and he put the needs of the bank and his longtime partners first, but he was left with little to nothing from his creation.

LESSONS LEARNED

- Bankers were not immune from the ravages of the Great Recession.

- The banks have to watch out for their balance sheet, just as any business does.

- The banking relationship is based upon trust.

- Banks are also susceptible to governmental regulations and penalties.

CHAPTER 15

LOSING IT ALL WITH MEZZANINE FINANCING

"He looked at me, squinted his eyes, and said,
'You sure there's nothing you want to tell me?'"

At least two of the CEOs interviewed for this book lost everything when they overleveraged their companies using mezzanine financing. The irony is that in both cases the entrepreneurs used that kind of financing for acquisitions and expansion of otherwise solid and profitable businesses.

In Chapter 9, we profiled Brad Adams, who described the tumultuous acquisition of an injection molding plant by his long-standing wire-stamping company. After years of crisis management, just as Brad received letters of intent to buy his company, his mezzanine lender forced it into bankruptcy. There was no reason for the mezz lender to do that, and it wiped out millions of dollars of value that would have benefited the lenders, including the mezz lender itself.

PHOENIX PRESCHOOLS

Michael Koffler has made and lost several fortunes over the past few decades, and he relied on mezzanine financing to fuel his aggressive growth strategy. A hardworking and smart entrepreneur in the New York City area, Michael was fresh out of college and selling insurance in the late 1970s, just as his wife had finished earning her credentials as a speech therapist. On the basis of his wife's occupation, they built several businesses related to speech and other therapies to help children and the elderly.

> New York–based Michael Koffler graduated from the University of Buffalo and went on to build or acquire more than sixty for-profit schools nationwide. YPO member.

Michael explained: "A guy my wife had worked for called her up and said, 'Maybe you should provide some therapists to a preschool.' That turned into creating our own preschool.

"It started in 1986, when other problems relating to an earlier business were crashing around my ears. We built a special-education preschool that was really tiny, and soon it was producing money, and I was feeling good. In 1988 I started another school like the first one; then a year later I added a third school. I continued with these three for another nine years.

"Later I started buying day-care centers, like KinderCares. I don't usually read the *Wall Street Journal*; however, one day I just happened to pick one up, and I saw a notice of a bankruptcy sale of seven day-care centers in Florida. After a few months of due diligence and research in 1994, I ended up buying those seven sites, which were in a very different environment from a big urban metropolitan area. From then until the summer of '98, I bought places that fit the right description.

"Basically, these little businesses would average $500,000 of revenue. Typically, they would have two hundred kids and twenty employees. Ultimately, I opened up in forty locations—twenty-one in North Carolina, four in Georgia, and fifteen in Florida."

LICENSING AND PERMITTING

Michael went on to describe what made all that fall apart: "A couple of the sites were in Pensacola. When you get a site relicensed, the licensing people have an opportunity to say that you need to upgrade something in this building. The fire department came in and said we needed to have more fire protection.

"I had a maintenance guy, and he brought in somebody from Lowe's. They measured the whole place and said it was going to cost $30,000 for Sheetrock. We measured it five times, and the price was all set. I put up a deposit of half the money.

"Two months later, as we got closer to the delivery date, the maintenance guy said he'd made a mistake. It turned out that I needed twice as much material and the cost of the material—which was wrong, too—was actually double what I'd been quoted. The price rose from $30,000 to $120,000.

"I found a supplier of Sheetrock from New York who was a good buddy of mine. We measured the place again, and it turned out that the original $30,000 estimate was wrong; we actually needed *less* material. I got all of it for $20,000 from my New York supplier. I sent it down to Florida and told the Lowe's guy to keep the deposit as liquidated damages but would not do any more business with him. He was angry.

"The years passed, and every three or four months you'd have an inspection from a day-care inspector. They'd come along and measure the rooms; they'd make sure you had enough toys; they'd make sure the teachers had examinations, a physical on file, and so on. That's normal pretty much all over the country.

"In July 1998, a mom came into the school and said something was wrong with her child. She asked a teacher to look at the kid's behind, but the teacher said, 'We're really not equipped to do that; you need to bring your child to a doctor.' This went on for three days.

"On a Friday night, I got a call from my regional manager who told me she and the program director were both in jail; they got arrested because the child who was complaining that there was something in his butt had finally gone to a doctor, which is what we told him to do. The doctor said that there was some abrasion on the child's butt. The day-care inspector, who came along every three or four months, accused my two employees and the doctor of neglecting to report a case of suspected child abuse.

"After an investigation, the conclusion was that this four-year-old boy was being 'vetted' into a club. We had an after-school program where there were kids as old as eight or nine, and a nine-year-old apparently took a stick or an acorn and stuck it in this little kid's behind. The police accused our school of not supervising things. They accused the program director, the regional director, and the doctor of not reporting this child-abuse incident, and evidently the day-care inspector orchestrated the entire event.

"The punch line is that the day-care inspector was the wife of the jerk from Lowe's who was so pissed off.

"I said, 'Oh my God, I can't take this.' I sold all the places. It took about three months, but I sold them all, and I started refocusing my attention on building more large-scale private schools in the New York area."

BUILDING NEW SCHOOLS

Michael continued, "It took about a year to figure out the first project, a nursery school meant for the high-end market. The New York community has a disproportionately large number of people who want to send their kids to private schools of their choice. I built one on the Upper West Side; it happened to take off really well, and after about three years, it was fully enrolled. It was about a $5 million business with EBITDA of about 22 percent. My next school was a high-end private school for children who had speech and learning disorders. That became successful also.

"The private school community around New York is filled with people who are attached to the school that they graduated from, and they want their kids and grandkids to go there, too. I decided to build a traditional private school. I figured that if I could attract the best staff and build an amazing campus, that it would work.

"So I scoured the city, and the best real estate arrangement I was able to make was in the Wall Street area, across from the Stock Exchange. I leased an old bank—a 125,000-square-foot building that had been vacant for fourteen years—whose owner was willing to invest $22 million in renovations. He did a terrific job.

"We built an amazing, beautiful building. I put a pool in the basement; we turned the old vaults into a cafeteria. I raised the roof and put a gym on top and an outside gym on top of that. Then I'm not sure exactly why I did this, but I decided to build a middle school and a high school. I did that as a building within a building, two blocks away on Broadway. We took 200,000 square feet, and I got another landlord to do another $20 million project at his expense. The site was awesome—gorgeous and amazing.

"On the other side of town, I built a really large private school for kids who had autism diagnoses. We originally built that place to hold 240 kids; the annual tuition was going to be $100,000, which is competitive even though it sounds really expensive. We started in the beginning with an enrollment of fifty or sixty kids. There were about half who could afford to pay and another half who could afford a deposit. We were able to run the school cash flow even. When you have a kid with special needs, the public school is supposed to provide the services, regardless of how expensive they may be. However, a legal process has to approve you for funding.

"So you have a handicapped kid, there's stress to the nth degree, and on top of that you don't have money, because how many families even in New York City have $100,000 dollars to pay school tuition?

"As the school started to grow, the recession hit. So now, it was 80 percent who couldn't pay and 20 percent who could. Now this is not total insanity, because in the beginning the settlement of these cases was happening within a year. Later it migrated to two years, but you had a 99.5 percent success rate. Ultimately, you receive the money, but how do you cash-flow the debt service while waiting to be paid?

"At that point, I knew people who might be a lending source. So I called a YPO friend and told him that I needed to take on some debt or equity and could he refer me to someone. He said, 'You know, this is something I can do.' That was about four years ago. We did a mezzanine debt deal. I borrowed $14 million where the interest rate was supposed to start at 12 percent. The net proceeds after all the expenses were not enough. I was paying 15 percent interest, but it was very unsustainable. We couldn't grow, because all the money that we were earning, even with EBITDA of $5 million, was spent on interest payments and funding those receivables."

THE SEARCH FOR PRIVATE EQUITY

"I brought in an investment banker," Michael said, "and we spent weeks trying to find a replacement source of capital. We needed bank debt that would be 4 or 5 percent interest and mezzanine money that would be about 10 percent. We were trying desperately to figure this out and get rid of the guys that I'd started with four years earlier. We started with 280 private equity houses and boiled it down to about twenty, then did management presentations to those twenty firms.

"One of the last guys I was talking to as a prospective lender sent in somebody to do a background check on me. (I'd had this done before in other situations when I was doing other financings.) He asked me questions about the close of a business back in 1986. He looked at me, squinted his eyes, and said, 'You sure there's nothing you want to tell me?' Obviously, I smelled a rat. I said no.

"The very next day, that lending source canceled out. When they called me, they said, 'We have to talk.' Now that Internet search technology has changed so much, people can find twenty-five-year-old articles. He had uncovered an old Medicare issue I thought was completely resolved.

"Even in 2010 it wasn't possible to dig up those old articles. Four years earlier, when I'd obtained the mezz money, I went through the same kind of four-hour study on me. So I really didn't have any reason to think that there was anything more to this. I thought that I had done the right thing back then, and that I was doing the right thing now.

"But they were calling me damaged goods and a dishonorable guy. I just listened quietly, and I said, okay, I understand, and then that was that. Without that funding, I ended up losing four of the schools to these mezz lenders. This fiasco cost me $20 million—that's $20 million out the window. The good thing is that I will not ever do business with mezz lenders again.

"I risked too much. There are some people who call me an equity hog. They think I should have taken in investors for equity, and then I maybe wouldn't have risked all my personal resources. I'm not going to load on tons of debt and burn through my personal assets. Therefore, that's a lesson learned. I'm not going to do that again."

LESSONS LEARNED

- Understand that if you are leveraged enough to need mezzanine financing, perhaps you shouldn't do the deal. What is your exit strategy from the debt? If it requires optimism, be exceptionally careful.

- Consider giving up equity rather than using mezzanine financing.

- Mezzanine and private-equity investors run thorough background checks. You need to be honest and straightforward.

PART FOUR

BANKRUPTCY & WORKOUTS

CHAPTER 16

BANKRUPTCY LAWYERS— THEIR VIEW

"The problem with asset protection is that it involves losing a degree of control over your assets."

never thought there would come a day when I would have to retain a bankruptcy lawyer. In fact, I was so completely overwhelmed that, when it came time for me to hire one, I was desperate for someone to help me out of the morass of problems. The bankruptcy attorney I hired actually required that he be the quarterback of the process.

In this chapter, bankruptcy and asset-protection lawyers discuss the characteristics of entrepreneurs and, from their perspective, the biggest challenges that entrepreneurs face.

ASSET PROTECTION

Bill Lobel is a highly respected bankruptcy lawyer in Southern California. With his fees at about $800 an hour, he is also expensive. His advice to entrepreneurs starts with what needs to be done *before* there is any sign of problems.

Bill Lobel, a highly regarded bankruptcy attorney, attended law school at the University of Miami and practices in Newport Beach, California, at Lobel, Neue & Till.

Bill said, "I am a strong believer in asset protection, if it is done when you don't have any creditors coming after you. If you protect your assets before any issues appear, then the protection sticks. The problem with asset protection is that it involves losing a degree of control over your assets, so entrepreneurs must decide what level of control they are willing to give up.

"The point is that when things are good, go to the lawyer who understands this area of the law and have him look at your particular situation and figure out how to structure the business so that you get the maximum leverage if things were to go wrong."

CARVE-OUTS—REDUCE YOUR EXPOSURE

Jeff Verdon attended Boston University School of Law and specializes in asset protection in Orange County, California, with the Jeffrey Verdon Law Group.

Attorney Jeff Verdon is a renowned expert in asset protection, and he described how banks viewed that strategy and whether they saw it as hiding assets: "I think the banks have adjusted to asset-protection planning. If you have a $10 million estate and you're borrowing $2 or $3 million, then the bank is going to be fine with $2 million to $3 million of alternative assets to pay them back. But if you're borrowing $3 million, it doesn't mean you have to have the other $7 million sitting out there just waiting to be plucked out by some future creditor."

That seemed straightforward to me. In my case, I had $25 million in assets and a $5.6 million line of credit with Bank of America. I could have easily limited my exposure, rather than leaving the entire estate wide open.

A useful concept is to see this not as asset protection but instead as lifestyle protection, on a level similar to an IRA or 401(k). Entrepreneurs should look at this as their responsibility to their family to provide a consistent lifestyle, regardless of the success or failure of their business. It is just as important as a retirement plan, health insurance, or life insurance.

My former view of asset protection was that it was sneaky, that I would be hiding assets from banks and creditors. If I had seen it as a family responsibility and a method of ensuring our lifestyle, I would have been much more open to it. If you have personal guarantees, then you need to have highly restricted carve-outs limiting your liability and to have asset protection in place.

A DIFFERENT PERSPECTIVE ON ENTREPRENEURS

Len Shulman, the senior partner in a Southern California legal practice, specializes in bankruptcy. Perhaps uniquely, he not only represents entrepreneurs, he also is the counsel for banks, creditors, and bankruptcy trustees. Len straddles all sides of the fence, so to speak. He represented the bankruptcy trustee during my personal Chapter 7 proceedings; he was bright, fair, and communicated efficiently.

Len Shulman is a highly respected bankruptcy attorney who graduated from the University of San Diego School of Law. He is a senior partner at Shulman, Hodges & Bastian in Orange County, California.

Len shared his perspective on entrepreneurial traits: "I think there is a common theme among entrepreneurs who either find themselves in insolvencies or choose to voluntarily go in. First of all, they are huge risk takers. In fact, you could characterize some of them as downright gamblers.

"One of the terms that I learned early on actually comes from Bill Lobel, and it's what he calls the 'debtor syndrome.' It's this unusual amount—almost to a fault—of optimism, where you can't see the downside risk because you are so optimistic that something around the corner will take you over the hump when you're having some challenges.

"That's the same kind of characteristic you would find in chronic gamblers, because they believe they will win and stave off all the losses. That's when you know it's become an addiction. This uber-optimism is one of the characteristics of an entrepreneur who ultimately has to face the prospect of insolvency.

"Entrepreneurs are generally very well educated and articulate, and they need to be. They are either attracting financing or attracting intellectual capital from others to take the steps that they need to in an attempt to build their business. Another characteristic is that they tend not to be entirely transparent, because they feel that those around them might see chinks in their armor. I am not saying that the lack of transparency is criminal or nefarious in nature, it's just that they are guarded. Entrepreneurs are high achievers, so they like to be in control. They are a bit of a puppeteer in terms of orchestrating everything around them and making sure their environment is very controlled.

"Many entrepreneurs tend to overspend and are not overly concerned with a budget. They have the optimism that they will always be able to earn back whatever they spent. I don't want to generalize and say all entrepreneurs are like that. If they were more focused on budgetary issues or living below their means, would they ever be faced with insolvency? Maybe, if they had a regulatory or governmental issue, or if they had an unfortunate experience with a banking issue. But the entrepreneurs who find themselves truly faced with insolvency are often people who cannot live within a budget."

In fact, it seemed to me that about 20 percent of the entrepreneurs interviewed for this book seemed to have out-of-control spending issues and that generally if the entrepreneur were overspending, his business was overspending as well.

Len continued, "If I recall, you had some employees who weren't entirely honest; they were taking advantage of you guys. But that plays into internal optimism, because when you're an eternal optimist, you trust everybody. Entrepreneurs faced with insolvency-related issues sometimes find themselves there because they are so trusting of those around them.

"There are often external factors that cause trouble for entrepreneurs, even though they were cautious and conservative. Look at the economy: That threw in a lot of entrepreneurs who were probably doing all the right things, but they still found themselves in a bankruptcy."

Len shared his views on how the bankruptcy process affects a marriage: "Going through a bankruptcy will end a marriage more often than not. Because there is blame, there is stress, a spouse gets used to a lifestyle and money, and when it's no longer there, then all of a sudden the responsible partner is a shithead. So that just ends up blowing the whole thing up."

PERSONAL GUARANTEES AND CREDITOR PROTECTION

Len also addressed the issue of why bankers choose to pursue a personal guarantee and why they sometimes do not: "I think they vigorously pursue them for two reasons. One, they do it out of emotion when they are angry; or two, when they think that there is a clear path to getting paid. If there isn't that clear path because of some savvy asset protection and the cost benefit is such that it doesn't make any sense, then they won't pursue it, unless they are just emotional and want to hurt the borrower."

I asked Len how creditors, banks, trustees, and so on perceived entrepreneurs when they have creditor protection in place years before there's an issue. As a long time Boy Scout, I felt as though asset protection was an activity that less-than-ethical people did, similar to hiding assets.

He said, "That's not slimy at all, it's savvy. It's hard to get entrepreneurs to buy into asset protection because it's like an insurance policy. No one wants to buy life insurance. No one wants to have to buy all these different insurances. Asset protection is another insurance policy in case things go bad. Getting entrepreneurs to buy into yet another layer of insurance is tough. But it's not viewed as slimy in the least. I think in this day and age, in light of outside forces, having an asset-protection plan is certainly recommended."

LEN'S ADVICE

"Number one, live under a budget. Live below your means. You may have a high budget, compared to mine, but live below your means. If you're making $1 million a year, make sure that you set aside $500,000 for taxes, and then spend less than $500,000 a year. Live under your means!

"Number two, truly vet, understand, and evaluate those around you to make sure that you're surrounding yourself with trustworthy people of like objectives. Surround yourself with people you know are going to reach your objectives and have your best interests in mind. Don't buy into your own press or feed off of your success. Continue to challenge yourself on whether or not what you're doing is the correct path. Be critical of yourself. If you are self-critical, and you have surrounded yourself with really good people, then you're probably going to stay on a good path, unless an outside force affects you.

"When it comes to dealing with banks, there are also legal strategies. If I were representing an entrepreneur with the bank, I would recommend open, honest transparency. I would ultimately recommend that the guarantor go what I call 'four paws up,' and stipulate to a judgment with a very, very modest payment stream for a long period of time. Then what happens over time is the bank's management will change. Ultimately, you can end up paying the judgment off at a steep discount.

"I have a client who ultimately stipulated into a judgment because the bank wanted to have press clippings. He stipulated to a $20 million judgment, and the payments were $200 a month, and he paid the bank every month for several years. Ultimately, he was able to pay the thing off after five years for $20,000 because the lien wasn't worth anything. New management didn't even want to do the administrative work of collecting the $200 every month."

LESSONS LEARNED

- Protect assets early, before there is a problem.

- Asset protection is not unethical or slimy; it is a responsibility of an entrepreneur, like retirement planning or life insurance. It's lifestyle protection, not asset protection.

- Banks perceive asset protection as sophisticated entrepreneurial financial planning.

- Negotiate carve-outs from personal guarantees. Don't over-guarantee a loan.

- Live within your means and according to a budget.

- Bankruptcies often end in divorce. Be prepared for marital woes if you're going into a bankruptcy.

- Be transparent with creditors. Agree to "four paws up"—an early judgment with low monthly payments for a long term. After five years or so, negotiate a settlement to pay it off for pennies on the dollar.

CHAPTER 17

WORKOUT STRATEGIES

"When someone files bankruptcy,
he is no longer the quarterback. I had to look
in the mirror to find the quarterback."

Entrepreneurs who experience severe financial duress have different approaches to and philosophies about handling creditors and the bankruptcy process. This chapter describes their strategies and experiences.

Software CEO Bob Verdun's prepackaged Chapter 11 bankruptcy in 2001 was described earlier in the book. He went into further detail about what followed: "I really did not set myself up with a high probability of success after the bankruptcy. For several years, sales were nearly flat with little net profit due to aggressive repayment of debt to creditors.

"I had way too much debt on the business coming out of the bankruptcy. We had been the rock stars of our industry before we crashed. I really thought that if the word got out that we were in trouble, everything would all come crashing down. In hindsight, I probably would have been better off financially to flush the whole thing, start a new company, and trust that the customers would follow. But I really felt like these were my obligations and my debt, so I should figure out how to pay them back. I was kind of torn, but that is the path that I chose, and that's the end of it.

"Before the bankruptcy, we had a schoolboy optimism about everything—a limited financial reporting system and lack of controls. There are a hundred different things that I learned through the process that made me a better businessperson by an order of magnitude."

THE $1 MILLION SACRED COW

Earlier in the book, we profiled Richard, the anonymous CEO of a Southern California home-building business that the Great Recession crushed. He was better prepared than most, but he still lost most of his fortune. He passed along some advice about dealing with tough lenders:

"I would say to a creditor, 'I've got obligations to other lenders, surety bond holders, and investors.' And I explained to the creditors that when things go bad and there's no more money coming in, I have to have enough working capital for eighteen months to close this thing up and finish filing tax returns. I have obligations to these LLCs and the partners and such. So to wind all that down, I've got to be able to fund everybody for eighteen months; I need to reserve those funds. I made the money a sacred cow, saying, 'You are not touching that. You want to fight? We'll fight, okay?'

"It's not that I want $1 million because I want $1 million. It's that I have $1 million reserved because I have an obligation to partners. I have to fulfill these obligations, and that's what it takes. And I never mentioned the bankruptcy word; everybody knew what we were talking about.

"I used many analogies when speaking with creditors, but I always found it better not to mention the word 'bankruptcy' in these negotiations. That's actually advice that [bankruptcy counsel] Bill Lobel gave me, advice that I think has served me well."

BUILDING ALTERNATIVE REVENUE

Richard continued, "The process for me was finding a way to build and maintain an eighteen-month reserve so I could meet the challenge I found myself in. Others think you're depleting the reserves; hopefully you're not. To reach the goal, you begin flipping houses or finding other new opportunities for some revenue. You do everything possible to cover your overhead, so you're not chipping away at that cash balance.

"You know, it's a balancing act. If you can generate income and revenues to cover your overhead, then you're saving the reserve, whereas maybe before you'd invest in equity and real estate deals. Now you're only doing first-trust deeds at conservative loan-to-value rates, and things like that. So it's a different risk profile but it helps, and it adds to that benefit of keeping the $1 million reserve in place, covering the overhead and allowing you more runway space.

"You just try to get through the valley until the entrepreneurial opportunity turns into a business opportunity you can utilize to legitimately pay for your overhead and give the business a wealth-building strategy.

"When someone files bankruptcy," Richard said, "he is no longer the quarterback. I had to look in the mirror to find the quarterback. I felt it was best for me to remain in control of the process. I hired two different bankruptcy attorneys, even though I never had to file, and I got second opinions on things like taxes. I looked at this as though I were going to graduate school or completing a doctoral dissertation. I had to dig in, I got on the Internet, and started reading case law on bankruptcy."

Richard spent a couple years negotiating through his creditor issues. He landed squarely on his feet and preserved a decent portion of his assets. He could have filed for bankruptcy. He could have entered into litigation. Instead, he chose to methodically settle with each creditor.

LESSONS LEARNED

- Doing a prepackaged Chapter 11 is possible if you have enough cash and a new money source.

- Sometimes it is better to liquidate the old company, and start fresh with a company that has a healthy balance sheet.

- Do not evaluate the business alternatives with nonrealistic optimism.

- When meeting with creditors, do not threaten bankruptcy directly. It is often more professional to hint at bankruptcy rather than use it as a threat.

- In a workout, reserve a specified cash balance that will be needed to unwind the company in case of business failure. The cash balance can then be invested as working capital to keep the core staff working through the tough times.

- If you set aside a reserve cash balance, try to preserve it through smart investing focused on positive cash flow.

- At the end of the day, you are the person responsible for making it through tough times. Obtain advice and assistance from staff, attorneys, accountants, and others, but remember, it is your future at risk.

CHAPTER 18

THE COMPLEXITIES OF ASSET PROTECTION

"Entrepreneurs will not take action to protect themselves and their families so that recessions can't wipe them out."

As Richard, the anonymous CEO of a Southern California home-building company, observed, "Entrepreneurs will not take action to protect themselves and their families so that recessions can't wipe them out." This chapter reviews the need for asset protection in greater detail, along with the concept of lifestyle protection and the entrepreneur's responsibility to protect the family.

A HARMFUL MIND-SET

Richard went on to say that entrepreneurs believe that "asset protection is important but not urgent, so the tendency is not to invest in it right now. You know about it, but it's filed in a drawer where you store it or compartmentalize it and think you'll pull it out when you need it.

"So entrepreneurs fail to plan properly. They imagine an 'I can get into any mess and land on my feet' scenario. They think, 'I hear what people are saying, but I've got this business to run. I've got all this stuff to get done, and I'll deal with it later.'

"Entrepreneurs have got to get over this mind-set."

And if business owners tell their financial advisors not to worry about creditor protection—as I foolishly did—Richard pointed out that advisors need to look entrepreneur clients squarely in the face and say, 'What percentage of creditor or liability risk are you worried about? Is there a possibility of a 10 percent risk? Twenty percent?'

He continued, "You know there is more than zero risk of a creditor liability, even if you *don't* have your own business. Anyone can have a serious car accident or other liability that is in excess of insurance. So a financial advisor has to get an assessment out of the entrepreneur. If there is a 20 percent chance this might happen, shouldn't you take that into consideration and protect assets? Because most of us consider the risk is low, we think we don't have to worry about it. But you have to plan for that risk."

LIMITED PROTECTION

Mike Brown, the former CEO of his family's Arizona-based home-building business, knew his father had established a trust fund for him. Therefore, Mike had established trusts for his own kids. His dad had also raised him to diversify assets and not use leverage too much. But even with all this as a framework, there were lessons to be learned.

Mike talked about the complexities of asset protection: "You've got to be careful. Asset protection can become a full-time job in itself. I've had resources for years to help with asset protection. But advisors and attorneys don't always tell you the whole story. For instance, consider LLCs. If you are a single-asset LLC, it's not that protected. If you've got a charging order, for example, you're going to lose."

In my case, even before I sold MuniFinancial, I had established a complex group of corporations, LLCs, and limited partnerships to contain all the assets within my estate. But since I owned 100 percent of the entities, the court pierced them in a single court hearing with no discussion. The entities that I thought would provide some creditor protection were worthless, since they were set up for liability protection instead.

CHILDREN'S TRUSTS

In the early 1990s I had established an irrevocable children's trust for my daughters, and I spent considerable time developing an appropriate structure for it. I had moved about 20 percent of the stock from my first company, MuniFinancial, into the children's trust a few years before selling the business. Because of the minority interest, the stock value reduced significantly, allowing us to transfer that amount with limited tax consequences. When I sold MuniFinancial, we were able to move a couple of million dollars into the children's trust, and for many years the kids benefited from the trust.

However, I irresponsibly included the children's trust in my personal guarantees. There was no good reason for me to do so. It was just a stupid call on my part, one of many decisions that I regret. So although the irrevocable children's trust can be an effective tool, I violated its effectiveness. Other entrepreneurs profiled in these pages had irrevocable trusts that remained in place without impact, because they kept those trusts separate from the rest of their estates.

PRENUPTIAL AGREEMENTS AND DIVORCE

Mike Brown had a prenuptial agreement with his wife, which allowed him to take on liabilities without including her assets and provided another layer of protection to their estate. Other more risk-oriented entrepreneurs that I spoke with also had prenuptial agreements and specifically kept their spouses off any personal guarantees. One entrepreneur mentioned that he actually had divorced his wife to separate and protect property from creditors, only to remarry her later after the dust settled.

When I married again in 2014, my wife and I entered into a prenuptial agreement. Heather and I are both entrepreneurs, so it made sense for us to protect one another from any potential liabilities.

LIFESTYLE PROTECTION

Alejandro Rivas Micoud, the Spanish telecom and technology entrepreneur, had some useful thoughts about protecting assets after a sizable payday: "I would advise anybody who makes it big to put aside enough of their estate to enable them to live at their basic quality of life in case everything goes to hell—that way they won't lose everything."

He acknowledged, however, that it's difficult for entrepreneurs to do so, "because they're that kind of person. They became wealthy probably because they were risk takers in the first place, so it is a good bet that they'll keep on taking risks. If they do that, and they lose everything, it's good to have put away just enough to continue having a basic living standard. That's something that I didn't do or didn't do enough of, I guess. In my next life I'll do it better."

Dan Stephenson, CEO of Rancon Development, had lost his wealth several times due to recessions, but he admitted he never created a start-over fund or maintained substantial reserves.

He said, "I feel I should have done it but never did. In the last up cycle, I committed to putting $20 million in stocks and diversifying outside the real estate business, whether it was stocks or bonds. Unfortunately, I drink my own Kool-Aid, and I have confidence in what we do. Every time I turned around, I was buying more of what I really understood. I'd think, 'How can I turn $100 million into $200 million, and that into a billion?' That's the mind-set you get."

INSURANCE AND CASH FLOW

The issue of insurance only came up once during the thirty interviews with other entrepreneurs, but my own experience leads me to include it here. When my world at TurnKey started to unwind, and creditors filed lawsuits, I asked our CFO about the status of our directors and officers (D&O) insurance. Keep in mind that we were spending far more than a million dollars a year on different liability insurance products. We had to have design errors and omissions insurance since we provided architectural services; we had building-defect insurance, construction insurance, general liability insurance, and directors and officers insurance, just to name a few.

Unknown to my COO and me, the CFO had canceled our D&O insurance a year earlier because cash flow was tight. I regretted that decision for a decade afterward.

If the CFO had left the D&O policy in place, instead of creditors suing me personally, I could have filed a D&O insurance claim, and I could have avoided years of litigation, expense, and heartache.

Similarly, Jim Glazer, the Nebraska-based specialty-truck CEO, had reduced his company's liability insurance when his cash flow tightened around 2004. A year later, there was an accident at an airport involving one of their trucks. The lawsuits started, and Jim realized that they were underinsured.

It cost the company severely. He spent years litigating the matter and ended up paying a huge settlement. As we all know, the check you write may be significant, but the true cost of legal wrangling is the lost opportunity of growing your organization. Litigation sucks the energy out of the top producers. Jim now carries appropriate insurance, and he considers it a foundation of the company.

LESSONS LEARNED

- Lifestyle protection needs to be now, not later. Asset protection needs to be set up when there are no problems. You never know when an external event can strike.

- Drop the investor thinking for any assets set aside for lifestyle protection. If you are earning less with those assets, that's OK. You need a risk-manager mentality, not an investor mind-set.

- Make sure any entities created for asset protection have multiple assets and owners. Single assets and owners may not provide appropriate protection.

- Irrevocable trusts are effective, but make sure never to use them for guarantees.

- Prenuptial agreements can also be effective to protect assets and keep your spouse from liabilities.

- Avoid reducing your investment in liability insurance when cash flow is tight. Dropping insurance can end up costing millions of dollars and years of heartache.

PART FIVE

PERSONAL CHALLENGES & LESSONS

CHAPTER 19

NOW THAT YOU'VE MADE IT

*"Even when other investors stopped throwing
more money in, Dale kept doling it out."*

An entrepreneur's optimism needs to be balanced with risk management, but that doesn't always occur. This chapter covers common mistakes made after a large liquidity event, such as the sale of your business, and reviews the importance of creating a vision and plan for your life and wealth.

Dale Jensen and his partner were pioneers in computer systems for the banking industry back in the early days of computers. They founded Information Technology, Inc. (ITI), which was involved in automating small and medium-size banks. Ultimately, the firm grew to about $90 million in sales and 800 employees. In the mid-1990s, they sold it to Fiserv, a financial services company, after which Dale had a one-year consulting contract.

WHAT'S YOUR PLAN?

Dale had a huge payday. He wanted to use his wealth to help his friends' dreams come true, much as his had. He started putting millions of dollars into "investments" that his friends presented. In addition, he invested in projects in which he had little expertise. For example, he bought the largest farm in Minnesota (26,000 contiguous acres) from the RTC and annually reinvested, hoping that it would return a profit someday. It never did.

Dale Jensen, an early pioneer in banking technology, grew his company, ITI, to $90 million in sales and 800 employees, and sold it to Fiserv in the 1990s. He then diversified into numerous investments, including several high-profile real estate developments and sports team ownership.

"I had a couple of businesses in which I kept throwing good money after bad," Dale remembered, "trying to save some of the investments I had with people I knew. I had to do something. You just can't stop everything. I lost my father in '97, when I was in my forties, and I was a lost soul for a while. I didn't have any base—it wasn't a stable family situation."

Dale then moved to Phoenix and looked for projects in that area. He ended up being a significant investor in the LLCs for two professional sports teams, the Suns and the Diamondbacks. As such, he had some ownership but no control. When the teams were losing money, and the managers were asking for funds, he had to put in additional capital. Even when other investors stopped throwing more money in, Dale kept doling it out.

He then looked at becoming an active developer in the downtown Phoenix area. He worked with the city and other agencies on a huge, expensive entertainment complex. He invested in things that, while grandiose and exciting, were out of his area of expertise. In the end, he lost tens of millions of dollars and came close to having to file personal bankruptcy.

WHAT WORKED ONCE MAY NOT WORK TWICE

A brilliant entrepreneur, Patrick van den Bossche was CEO of a modular-trailer-building company backed by venture capital and located in California. Patrick aggressively grew the company, then sold it to a publicly traded modular company. In the sale, he netted about $10 million in the new company's stock, but he felt there was little purpose to his career after the sale.

Patrick van den Bossche graduated from Cal Poly Pomona with a degree in architecture. He grew his modular-trailer manufacturer to a national platform and then successfully sold the company. YPO member.

Although Patrick still had a voice in the company, he was no longer the leader of the company, and it seemed that no one was listening. He also felt disconnected from family and friends; he had strained the relationship with his wife severely over the years of growing and selling his company. Ultimately, he met a dynamic woman from Arizona named Denise with whom he fell in love, and he initiated what turned into a messy and costly divorce.

He wanted to be done with his marriage as quickly as possible and said that, for his wife, "The divorce came as a surprise. She didn't want to get a divorce; I just wanted to make it clean. I told my attorney that I would write a check. By this time, I could sell stock, so I did. I wrote her a check for more than $5 million, all against the wishes of my attorney.

"I remember thinking to myself, 'It's a lot of money, but you know what, I can do this. I think it's fair.'"

Unfortunately, the value of his remaining stock shares soon sharply decreased. Patrick married Denise and moved to Arizona, where Denise happened to have a small modular building company that she operated largely by herself. She and Patrick discussed having him help her grow her small business into something huge.

He remembered, "At first, Denise was just terrific and said she loved me being involved, growing her company. What I didn't understand was that I was trampling on her baby. At the end of the day, it wasn't about the fact that she had a $100,000-a-year business. It was about the fact that she had created something, and I was, in essence, pissing all over it.

"I had set out the way I've always set out. I just pushed her to the side. She went willingly, but it created a fair amount of problems. In my mind, I was going to build a $10 million . . . $20 million business. That's what I'd done before, and I was going to do it again. It was a similar business, I'd been so successful before, why wouldn't all those things work on this, right?

"I completely ignored that it was a different sector with different economics and different business drivers. I started building out the team. I didn't understand that the business did not need some positions. I didn't need a CFO. I only needed to have a part-time finance person.

"In retrospect, we shouldn't have tried to scale the business. That was the secret: We should have run it out of our house. It would have been more successful. Nevertheless, we tried to make it big. I built an entire business plan; the only thing missing was the revenue.

"I said, 'We'll finance this—I'll get from here to there. I've got the history book for how it happens. Don't worry, Denise, I've been down this road. It's scary, but trust me, I've got the experience.'

"So we took on some loans to grow the business. And when the lenders needed a personal guarantee, I said, 'No problem,' because that was small potatoes for me.

"Now I understand that a personal guarantee doesn't mean you're just going to be on the hook for $100,000 or $200,000, but I had opened the door to something about the size of the Grand Canyon."

Patrick ended up having to take the company through bankruptcy. He has huge regrets about hurting his wife's enterprise, but he reinvented himself in other industries, and they remain happily married.

LIFE IN THE FAST LANE

Brian Lesk was the owner and CEO of the largest employee-leasing company west of the Mississippi, a stable business built on long-term recurring revenue. As an intelligent, experienced entrepreneur, he had survived difficulties during Y2K and was able to enjoy the firm's wild growth from 2001 through 2007.

Brian also loved to have fun and was very generous. Since his business was throwing off huge amounts of cash, and he had no wife, kids, business partners, or board of directors, he lived life in the fast lane. His personal spending, at its peak, was about $250,000 per month. He enjoyed his jet, homes around the world, and frequent excursions that might cost $50,000 for a weekend.

The lack of accountability also led him to make investments in deals he knew nothing about, including some with home builders and developers.

All of that came to a head in 2008, as the economy came to a screeching halt. Brian had no liquidity, and he lost the goose that laid the golden egg to a lender whom he brought into the business. It was a painful lesson. Brian now values his lifestyle and money more than he did in his heyday. He has much less than before, but what he has is more meaningful to him.

LESSONS LEARNED

- When you have a large payday, develop a financial plan for the proceeds, and integrate lifestyle protection into that plan.

- Do not invest in other businesses with your proceeds. If you want to act as an angel investor, use a small portion of your funds and limit the investment to those dollars.

- Best practice is to not lend money to friends.

- If you made it big once, do not assume automatically that you'll do it again. If you are going to be a serial entrepreneur, use other people's money on the next venture, limiting your personal exposure. Preserve your personal capital.

- Be careful of the uber-optimism that is characteristic of entrepreneurs.

CHAPTER 20

RIDING THE WAVE ONTO THE SAND

*"True happiness involves basically three things—
something to do, someone to love,
and something to hope for."*

Sometimes, as entrepreneurs, we lose a balanced perspective and forget what is important in life. This chapter covers common issues related to unbridled optimism and loss of perspective.

DREAMS OF GOING PUBLIC

By 1999 a competitor of Alejandro Rivas Micoud had gone public. The company had about the same size and market position as his firm. He discussed the effect on him and his business.

Alejandro Rivas Micoud earned his MBA from INSEAD and became a telecom entrepreneur. He bought, ran, and sold several telecom companies and had been offered as much as €400 million for one of them, netting him €40 million personally. YPO member.

"They went to market, got listed at a valuation of $1 billion, and immediately it jumped up to $6 billion," said Alejandro. "This really made our parent company very keen to do the same. We contacted Morgan Stanley and Goldman Sachs, and they said, 'Yeah, you guys can go to market, no problem.' They valued us at €1.6 billion. We started to prepare for an IPO.

"I wanted Goldman Sachs, but unfortunately my parent company went with Morgan, which was a mistake. The bankers at Morgan advised us to buy some downstream distributors to present a more coherent story for the IPO. Of course, that may have made sense from a narrative perspective, however, it saddled us with a lot of fixed cost. And it turned us from a positive EBITDA into a negative EBITDA situation. Morgan told us that it was not an issue, because really what investors wanted to see was growth of net profitability.

"We had just been awarded a mobile broadband license, and we had two great Spanish industrial companies as partners for that market. Our bankers advised that with the growth of data you really need to have an exchange-carrier type of strategy. You know, digging up the streets, putting in tubes, and doing all that stuff. Unfortunately, we accepted their advice. At the time, I was young and naïve. Whenever we met with an investment banker, I thought those guys were very suave and debonair. They sounded really smart. It took me a while to realize they were just salesmen."

DISTORTION

Alejandro went on, "It was a very interesting year for me because on paper I thought that I was worth 10 percent of the valuation we were given, basically €160 million. Our consortium partners wanted to buy all my stakes, and perhaps half of them at a valuation of around €400 million. I might have gotten between €20 million and €40 million in the deal. For me at the time, the offer was peanuts; I wouldn't even consider it.

"From my very distorted point of view, I was worth more than €160 million. I thought we were going to go public and then there would be a pop in value so it would go six or seven times greater. I thought I was standing at the border of €1 billion of net asset.

"The bubble popped, and when it did, the IPO was canceled. I met with my parent company in New York, a global telecom organization. It was very clear to me that boat was sinking, and it was strictly a matter of time. The main investor in the parent company put in some additional money but not enough to save the boat. I started looking around for ways to buy out the Spanish entity and convinced two Spanish companies to partner with me in a three-way bid, where they would provide the funds for my part of the stake.

"We offered €450 million for the Spanish company in August 2000, but the parent company did not accept the bid. Two months later it changed its mind. They came back to us and said they would like to accept the bid, but by that time my partners were no longer interested.

"I put together a second bid that valued everything at €250 million. Again, the parent company didn't accept, only to change its mind at the end of the year. I then put together a final bid with a gas company in Spain, valuing the company at €80 million.

"When the parent company received that bid for €80 million, it was so shocking that it decided then and there, 'That's it. We're done.' They put it into the equivalent of Chapter 7; basically, they wanted to walk away and forget about the whole thing.

"When that happened in March 2001, my company was no longer cash-flow positive. In fact, because of the construction of fiber and all that, it was cash-flow negative to a tune of around €6 million a month. The company was saddled with debt of approximately €150 million. At the time, telecom was definitely not the flavor of the month, so the possibility of getting new equity investors was nil.

"In exactly twelve months, I went from believing that I had a company worth between €160 million and €1 billion, to believing it was worth zero.

"The year had been extraordinarily stressful because paper wealth was being destroyed each month. I experienced incredibly painful narcissistic blows, if you will. But then I felt such a sense of relief once it reached zero. My feeling then was, okay, I've hit the bottom; from here on there's only up.

"I truly felt that way. It was like a burden had been taken off my shoulders; I had nothing left to lose and everything left to gain. I convinced my employees and key management to see if we could survive for a few months just for the heck of it, just to be able to walk away and say we left a tiny thing behind us. We just didn't let everything crumble. We put up some resistance. It wasn't a huge business, but it was there. In 2001, I put together a management buyout offer and bought the company from the liquidators for €1."

THE €1 ACQUISITION

Alejandro continued, "We only had €4 million cash in the bank, and we had a burn rate of €6 million. Nonetheless, that's when an interesting thing started happening. First, I had an extremely motivated team of people, and they became even more motivated as the months and then the years passed. We managed to bootstrap and survive for years. The second thing was the magic of working capital. When circumstances force you to focus on certain things, it's amazing how much money you can get out of a change in the way you manage working capital.

"I really enjoyed the next three or four years, because it was us against the world, and we managed. During that process, there was a subsidiary with a wireless license, and the subsidiary still had all these Spanish company shareholders. About a year later, they decided that entering telecom was a big mistake. They wanted to get back in the construction business. We had some big boardroom-level fights.

"By 2002 I had managed to buy them out for €2—their entire stake—because they thought it was worthless. Since we had already done it once, the second time it was easier to restructure the number of employees, the debts, and this and that. We knew exactly what to do."

"We survived on a series of miracles over the course of three years. Then there were no more tricks to pull out of the hat. But by 2006 wireless technology and the rest of the company became exciting enough to be bought out."

THE BIG PAYDAY

Alejandro said, "Between the two transactions, we got about €24 million, which at the time was about $27 million. When that deal was signed, I remember thinking, 'Wow, this is it! I've been working for this all my life; I mean, it's not the €1 billion, it's not a €160 million, but it more or less meets the goals I've always had for myself. So that's it, I'm done. Now I can do other stuff, things I always wanted to do but never had the time to do.'

"Actually, though, life was not so good, because right before this happened, I'd gone to this executive management course with a professor I really loved when I did my MBA. During this course, I became good friends with one particular CEO. In 2005, he had done an exit for a lot of money—enough to buy two Ferraris and a huge mansion.

"When I saw him after he had done his deal, he looked terrible! He looked depressed. One of the subjects under discussion in the course was the stress that can affect people who are working very hard and are accustomed to a certain lifestyle. Then all of a sudden, they have their exit, which they think is nirvana, but it turns out it is *not* nirvana.

"So I had a forewarning. I thought I was ready for what was about to come, but I was not.

"I didn't recognize it at the time, but I went into a deep depression. I had all kinds of problems with my wife, and we ended up separating. I did crazy things; I went off the rails. The conclusion I've drawn is that true happiness involves three things: something to do, someone to love, and something to hope for.

"If you sell your company, you just lost one of those three foundations to happiness: something to do. You may have also just lost something to hope for, because maybe that company was the basis of the hope in your life. All of a sudden, you've lost that, too. You may also have destroyed relationships with your loved ones, because you think you can walk on water; after all, you created this great success. Meanwhile, you're perhaps unconsciously not aware of the withdrawal symptoms that you're suffering from lack of adrenaline."

RIDING THE WAVE

"That certainly happened to me," Alejandro said, "and I started doing the kind of things that I always wanted to do—writing a novel, learning about the filmmaking business, and directing movies. During this time, the company where most of my net worth was tied up was not yet public.

"But then, in early 2007, it went public, and the value quickly went up by 60 percent or so over a few months. I had a six-month lockup, and about five months into the lockup it reached a peak, which just happened to be right before the financial crisis of July 2007. The peak doubled the amount of money that I had in there. A month later when my lockup expired, the stock value had drifted down significantly and then took a huge hit in month six, so much so that it went down to just above the value when they first did the deal: $27 million.

"Here's where stupidity kicked in. I was sure this financial crisis was a temporary thing. The company was going to recover, so I just insanely held onto that stock throughout the course of the next two or three years. It didn't go down in a straight line, but it basically went down to $1, wiping everything out.

"Along the way I decided to get back into business. But know this: If you're not hungry, and you're comfortable financially, depending upon the type of person you are, you may approach things in a less than perfect state of mind by not being as focused as you should be or as hardworking as you should be . . . by being too mellow.

"Basically, I threw away four to five million dollars. In a start-up, sometimes you're successful, and sometimes you're not. But I probably could have reduced the amount that I lost if I had managed better. I could have reduced it even more if I had not been the sole investor or gotten other parties involved who might have either advised me well, shared the losses, or both. I think by the early part of 2012 all my stock was either spent or destroyed. That kind of variability is a little bit crazy.

"I was talking to a friend of mine who just finished a stint as a CEO of a medium-size pharmaceutical company, and he's been in a corporate situation all of his life. He's thinking about becoming an entrepreneur, and I told him, 'Don't even think about it—don't do it.' Certainly there are fun and rewarding times, and I don't have any regrets about anything other than what happened with my wife and kids during the separation."

Alejandro is still married to his wife and enjoys spending time with his children. He is doing well and is on his way to rebuilding his wealth.

LESSONS LEARNED

- Investment bankers don't know your business as well as you do. If they recommend strategies that aren't compatible with your vision of the company, keep looking.

- When you lose enormous wealth, the value of each dollar becomes clear. Can the value of money be maintained without losing it? I hope entrepreneurs can figure this out.

- When you have little wealth, the return on your investment is important. When you have substantial wealth, focus on preserving it and not on the return on your investments.

- Diversify your investments. If you sell a company and are paid through the acquiring company's stock, make a plan to liquidate your position as soon as possible and develop a diversified investment portfolio.

- When starting up a new company, include outside investors. Use other people's money. If you are held accountable, you will better your performance and raise the bar. Manage your risk exposure.

- Maintain humility, and don't believe your own press. Preserve your relations with your family and spouse. That is the most important thing in the world.

CHAPTER 21

COLLATERAL IMPACT– FRIENDS AND FAMILY

"My dad and I didn't talk for almost four years."

Unfortunately, the impact of losing massive wealth ripples far beyond the loss of the business and money, often affecting family and friends. Typically, entrepreneurs, who are conditioned to the daily stress, strain, and uncertainty of leading a business are not empathetic toward spouses, families, and friends who are touched by the volatility of the business. The spillover is real and can create significant damage to the relationships. This chapter covers those consequences.

Mike Brown, the Arizona-based home builder, discussed the impact on his wife and father, among other things: "As entrepreneurs, we have thick skulls. I can handle stress and volatility, but it was very tough for my wife. She had enjoyed taking the plane to our house in Cabo San Lucas and going out with girlfriends every weekend, but that all changed. Socially, that was tough on her. She was anxious about when the free fall was going to stop. That lack of certainty on where we'd end up was also hard on her.

"For me the free fall was also tough to handle, but I internalize things like that—I deal with it, and I work on finding a solution to it. But for the family, it's just a scary ride. My wife had to get a job, and she's struggling with that, working part-time here and there. We had to switch our child's school last year. It's been difficult.

"My dad and I didn't talk for almost four years. One day I woke up and said, 'He's my father. He's eighty years old now; he's not going to be on the planet much longer.' My wife still took the kids to see my parents all the time. I wanted my kids to know their grandparents.

"So my dad and I had lunch. Four hours later, we got out a lot of our issues, and now I talk to him on a regular basis. That was important to me, and I think it was to him. I said, 'Look, I want to become your son again and not your business partner. I don't want to be that again. I would like to be just your son.' And we've accepted that.

"There were other impacts: I'm a firm believer in giving back to the community, and I was involved in a lot of boards—the March of Dimes, the Kay Foundation, and Not My Kid. I helped them raise money. Because of my losses, those boards suffered, too. I resigned from those boards because I didn't feel like I could contribute as I used to. It's been tough mentally for me."

Jim Glazer, the Nebraska-based specialty-truck manufacturing CEO, talked about what it meant to have his wife rejoin the work force during his company's worst times: "My wife ended up working as a CFO for a surety company about three years ago. She's very sharp, but she wasn't working full-time. With the kids going to college, she got a job that pays her very decent money. Her employment keeps her busy, and her income is very nice. One silver lining about losing this much money is that we haven't been required to pay taxes for a few years."

Matt Hagen, the building-products CEO, discussed the personal effects of the catastrophic events that almost took out their thirty-eight-year-old family business. At the height of the financial crisis in the winter of 2008, they managed to refinance their $65 million corporate loan in an industry that should never have been able to find a lender, but there were family consequences.

He said, "It was brutal. We were putting up all of our assets and doing what we needed to buy more time, hoping this thing survives. Meanwhile, my dad was on sleeping pills and antidepressants. I wasn't sleeping. I lost twenty pounds.

"During Thanksgiving of '08, my dad said to me, 'You need to explain to everybody why this is all going away and what we're going to do.' It was just incredible. I mean, everybody's face was pale. It was a terrible Thanksgiving!

"I had gotten married in the fall of '07 to a girl who had only known all the good stuff that I had and the fortunate life we led. Our lifestyle up to that point was amazing, but within a year and a half, we were in the midst of a possible bankruptcy and having everything wiped out.

"Ultimately, we had to sell as many personal assets as we could and leverage the property that represented my dad's lifetime achievement, a home he built on the site of our family's vineyard in California. It was a large house overlooking Silicon Valley, a retirement home that he was going to go live in, and it had a multimillion-dollar appraisal. That house was the culmination of my dad's life work.

"Everybody in our industry who knew our story was basically saying, 'You guys are done. You're never going to survive.' My dad totally believed that. He was preparing for bankruptcy, and my wife and I were going to have to move to a small manufacturing plant we wanted to hold on to. I would have to begin over again in rural Virginia, starting out as a plant manager. That was his plan for me."

Matt and his family business survived, however, and they are thriving today.

Alejandro Rivas Micoud insightfully described the impact on his family of losing huge sums of money.

He said, "At the first stage, the kids didn't really know; they were too young to understand. The situation had no effect on them at all. My wife saw me going through some tough times. She was always worried about things, but once it seemed that everything had been lost, it actually became a happy time for me. That's probably true for my kids, too, because at that point I still had an income. I didn't know how *long* I'd have the income, but it was there. We lived very well.

"The separation between my wife and me . . . that was horrible. In fact, it is something that I will always regret because of my kids. There's no doubt in my mind that both the hard times and the good times laid the seeds for everything that happened. Then, after my wife and I got together again, the next three or four years were very comfortable for my kids. When the value of the stock deteriorated, though, and things were not going well with the start-up, I didn't want to burden them with that worry, so I didn't. The issue was invisible to them.

"Once I shut down the company and we moved here to the United States, our house was not as nice as the houses we were used to in Spain. Also we had to sell one of our houses in Spain, so the kids started to feel some effects of the business problems.

"I think it's good for them to get a sense of the real world, and I'm not unhappy about it. And if I do manage to get things back on track, it would be great for them, because it would show the kids that when things go sour it doesn't necessarily mean the end of the world, you just have fight for it."

LESSONS LEARNED

- There is often a huge impact on your family and friends. Typically entrepreneurs are conditioned to stress, strain, and uncertainty, but spouses, family, children, and friends are more vulnerable to those feelings.

- If the relationship between family members has been damaged, try to make amends. They will always be your family.

- The impact on philanthropy is great when wealth is lost. Your ability to participate on boards and fundraise may be limited significantly.

- For spouses, gaining employment during trying times may be beneficial, since it can help refocus their energies; plus the income can be helpful.

- Keeping kids grounded through good times and bad is paramount. Children can learn many lessons about perseverance and hard work during times of crisis, as well as the true worth of a dollar.

CHAPTER 22

KEEP YOUR HEAD ON STRAIGHT

*"I was the asshole who didn't cash in his chips
when he had a big stack in front of him."*

Though entrepreneurs may be used to dealing with business ups and downs, amassing significant wealth and losing it can still take an emotional toll. This chapter covers some of the things the entrepreneurs learned from their personal challenges.

PERSONAL LOWS

Bob Verdun recollected his worst days back in early 2001: "It was actually during the bankruptcy, which was unbelievably stressful. I went from having growth every year and feeling like a rock star to my low point. I clearly remember leaving the office one day when it didn't look like it was all going to come together and grabbing staplers, paper, and paper clips, so that if I had to start over, I'd at least have office supplies. I started laughing. That's how bad it got.

"It was rough and had a huge impact on my confidence. It took years to shake off the feeling that I had blown it. Wondering why did I decline an offer for $20 million cash when I owned 100 percent of the firm with almost no debt? I went from that feeling to grabbing a bagful of office supplies. Only in the last few years, do I feel that I've shaken most of it off, most but not all of it.

"I felt like I blew it, like I played at the poker table a few hands too many; I was the asshole who didn't cash in his chips when he had a big stack in front of him. That's kind of how I felt for a long time.

"I remember taking a piece of paper and drawing a line down the center. On the right-hand side, I would put 'controllable'; on the left-hand side, 'out of your control.' Then I would try to separate all the stuff that I was worrying about into one of those two categories. For the items on the controllable side, I would think through what I needed to do: What was the action plan, and who was going to take care of it? On the uncontrollable side, I had to make myself acknowledge that I couldn't control it. I couldn't control whether Comerica Bank cut the check for payroll, right? So I really tried to separate the two to keep my head in the game."

GAME FACE

As CEOs, we are required to be actors. When you're at your lowest point and staring into the abyss, you cannot reveal your fears to your team members. You have to maintain your game face. Bob said a wise friend once said to him, "When a pilot has a bad day, everyone on the plane has a bad day!"

Bob went on, "I really tried to be good at hiding my feelings and fears. Unfortunately, I kept much of those bottled up inside of me, which is probably why I carried so much baggage for a while. But if I got bad news that day and was worried things were going to fall apart again, I would tell everyone that I was meeting with somebody off site, or close my doors, or say I've got a conference call. I had to get good at masking my feelings from the staff, because, while I, as the owner, see the whole chessboard, most of the staff doesn't and there's no way you can communicate everything.

"You've got to keep morale up; you've got to keep spirits up. The biggest factor is to keep working the problem. You can let emotion take over, but at the end of the day, the only help was working the problem."

I remember the feeling of being emotionally flooded when I was at TurnKey. Sometimes I felt as though the world was coming to an end. It was helpful to keep working through the issues one at a time.

HEALTH PROBLEMS

Jim Glazer had some serious health issues when his company nearly imploded in 2010. He said, "I was physically ill during those times. I'm not sure how much the stress contributed, but I guess it did.

"Two years ago I had Bell's Palsy; my face went numb, and half of it was paralyzed. It was terrible. Then I was in a trade show last year and became severely hypoglycemic. I was in a planning meeting and got disoriented; it turned out that I had a tumor on my pancreas."

WHAT MAKES YOU HAPPY

Alejandro Rivas Micoud discussed what he has learned about happiness: "The person who needs very little is in a better position than the person who has a lot. That sounds nice, but in reality, it's not a philosophy that most people follow.

"When I'm on top of the game, that's not necessarily my happiest moment. My happiest moments have been when I've been moving up— that's a great feeling. When things are improving, when I can see that we're getting places and I can see the possibility of a huge payoff, those moments are fantastic.

"When I'm playing the game, and it feels like I'm winning, that's great. When I finish the game, even if I won, that's not so great. My advice to anybody who is expecting a big payoff would be to really prepare something that is going to occupy their time in a very significant way and also have something that has an element of achievement to it.

"When that payoff day comes, and the goal is met, the letdown can be huge. I concluded that having an employment agreement for a couple years with the acquiring company is likely a very good way to make the transition. It keeps you in the game, it gives you an immediate purpose, and you are surrounded by people all day long who haven't made tens of millions of dollars. Therefore, it keeps you grounded and, hopefully, less narcissistic."

After I sold MuniFinancial in 1997, I had a two-year employment agreement. I never went through dark days after the sale, and I do believe that was part of the reason. It kept me engaged and in the game.

NO LONGER "THE GUY"

Patrick van den Bossche said, "My marriage really started feeling the pain that I had inflicted, not only within my family but also within my extended family. I didn't have kids, but my brothers and sisters and friends—everyone was a bit of a stranger to me. I had spent so much time growing the business, I had success, and I had the most net worth that I ever had, but I felt lonely.

"I internalized a lot, and it wasn't healthy. In '97 and '98, I felt alone, and I didn't feel meaningful in the business and the market. Before the sale, I hadn't just been CEO of the company, I had been 'the guy.' With the new company, I gained a voice, but I could have been speaking Dutch and it would have had the same result. After a couple of years, I thought I needed to do something different."

LIVE LIKE A REFUGEE

Richard, the anonymous CEO, said, "There were about eighteen months where I spent about three hours sleeping each night. I got to a point where I looked like a skeleton because I got to bed at 11 p.m. and I'd wake up at 2 a.m. If I got three hours of sleep, that was a pretty good night.

"I read a lot of books—business books, spiritual books, the Bible— thinking that after two, three hours of this, I'm going back to sleep. But I couldn't sleep. I'd get up about 5 a.m. and go for a run. I logged a lot of miles. Consequently, my pants were hanging on me, which, when I was negotiating with the banks, actually worked to my advantage. I looked a little gaunt, yet I was in pretty good health.

"I did have to manage the stress. The running was helping me. Physically, I was fit, but the stress . . . some of my friends had heart attacks and died. There were developers who behaved oddly under unmanaged stress. One guy in Las Vegas jumped off a balcony over a deal; another guy walked out after the bank told him they were going to come after him, and he pulled out a revolver. Another guy drifted out in the ocean on his yacht and jumped out and drowned.

"It all goes back to the self-worth thing. Remember, this isn't who you are. This is a component of your life or a chapter in the book.

"As hard-driving entrepreneurs, we all get a little overconfident. There is a bit of cockiness and swagger in us. But I think a lot of times there are moments, especially if you're YPO, where you have transparency and you are able to develop your relationships. It's important to have a 'realness' that allows you to develop relationships at high levels.

"I would have really gotten my ass kicked if I didn't have some friends who were running a major fund. I ended up putting out about $150 to $200 million, and I gave them some great deals. They became white knights who bought a number of my transactions and helped me facilitate deals and even acquired notes and ended up with my guarantees. You want guarantees in a friend's hands, not in a foe's. When people do not have those relationships, it makes a downturn so much more devastating."

NOT A BILLION-DOLLAR GUY

Dan Stephenson offered insights about knowing what you are really good at: "In 2005 my president said, 'We can make this a billion-dollar company.' But I am not a billion-dollar guy. I'm not a guy who can run an organization with thousands of people. That's just not my style. I am a really hands-on guy and a relationship guy.

"Every time my management team would say, 'We can own the Inland Empire,' we ended up broke, or I lost my net worth. And when we decided we wanted to be billionaires in the early 2000s, that's when we lost *all* of our net worth.

"I think you have to decide and really understand yourself and your style of management. I went to the Harvard executive MBA program. I went to USC. I went through YPO. And you try to learn all those lessons. But do you really learn them?

"How do you figure out what your strengths are? I think it's one of the real challenges. I loved what the president of my real estate company, Mike Diaz, said. 'If we had a problem in the real estate company, it's because I was constantly pushing them to open new offices and expand, so it could become worth more money.'

"Mike finally looked at me not too long ago and said, 'You know, all I want to do is be the best real estate manager I can be. I don't want to be a syndicator. I don't want to go buy real estate. I do not want to own buildings. I just want to run a real estate company.' He understands who he is and what he does, and, as a result, he runs an operation second to none. I do believe I had a hard time looking up and saying, 'What am I really good at?' and keeping it at that.

"Now that being said, the one thing I did do is the reason I survived with a great reputation. I decided we were only going to specialize in the Inland Empire, and we were not going to be a nationwide or state-wide real estate company. I believe that principle has kept us unique. It's the reason we survived this recession and why we will survive and grow rapidly in an upswing."

TAKE CARE OF YOURSELF

Don, the anonymous construction-equipment CEO, acknowledged that keeping his sanity when his business was in crisis was a huge challenge: "I was a single dad. When I had custody, I'd go home and make dinner for the kids. Kids have their own challenges and problems. In lieu of punching a hole in the wall or yelling at your kids, you've got to find ways to maintain your sanity. That might be the time for some exercise or to work out at the gym. I would often go jogging and scream at the top of my lungs some place where nobody could hear me."

At the peak of the stress during my TurnKey bankruptcy, I started doing intense yoga practices every day, about ten hours per week. It helped me physically and gave me the ability to keep my head on straight. Also, I lost the thirty pounds that the previous decade of long hours had added.

It also helps to talk to other people who have been through hard times. Mike McKeough had heard about the importance of caring for yourself physically. He had long periods of sleepless nights, and for months his right hand wouldn't stop shaking. He couldn't even hold a cup of coffee in his hands.

Mike said, "I guess a big thing I learned is that the business and financial stuff is brutal—it's tough—but it couldn't hold a candle to the anguish and the personal devastation from [my son's] boating accident. Business issues are a lot of work, but they're not nearly as devastating as the feared loss of my child, and the loss of his friend, and all the ramifications of that.

"I want to be happy. And the most important thing to me is to have happy and productive children. But the definition of productive is my kids' definition for themselves, not mine for them."

Mike isn't focused on having a $100-million personal net worth anymore. He wants to live comfortably and with security for himself and his family.

LESSONS LEARNED

- Create a list of the issues you're worried about. Separate them into Controllable and Uncontrollable. Develop an action plan for the Controllable. For the others, you have to realize you can't control them.

- Take care of yourself physically and emotionally. Whether you choose to run, go to the gym, or practice yoga, do something active every day. Meditate or attend church, spend time with family, and try to maintain a life outside of business.

- Think of difficult times as just a chapter in your life. Your career is only a part of you, it is not who you are.

- Know what you are good at, and try to keep it at that. Make a thoughtful assessment of your strengths and desires.

- If you have a successful exit with a nice payday, consider an employment contract with the company to help the transition. Otherwise, make sure to have active hobbies and a broader purpose, so that the sale of the company was just the attainment of one of the many goals in your life.

CONCLUSION

Each reader will undoubtedly take away different lessons after reading this book. I hope that this research and the experiences of the entrepreneurs profiled throughout lead you to actionable changes in one or more areas of your life or business. What I have learned is that, while there are risk factors associated with various companies, absent any planning and protections, all enterprises and entrepreneurs are subject to wildcard events that make them susceptible to financial disaster. No matter how smart you are or how stable you think your business is, you are at risk.

What I want to achieve through this book is to convince entrepreneurs to take the necessary steps to mitigate their risks and to protect their lifestyle for themselves and their families. This involves a multitude of changes, some small and some large. On the business side, it might include throttling back the growth of your company, converting to more recurring-revenue-oriented projects, balancing governmental funding with private-sector business, or hiring a well-qualified CFO and listening to him or her. From a personal perspective, actions could include setting aside a portion of your estate in gold, reducing your personal guarantees, creating a children's trust, or diversifying your investment portfolio.

We have developed a risk-assessment tool to help evaluate your individual and business risk. This is a self-assessment tool. It would be interesting to use it annually to measure your success in mitigating the risk to your personal estate and your business. We encourage you to use it as you think best. It is available online:

www.pathwaypartnersllc.com/risksurvey

Above all, I want to emphasize how important it is not only for you to understand the risks that we as entrepreneurs face in business, but also that we share that knowledge with those around us. That includes your leadership team, your YPO forum, your family, friends, and anyone else who has a stake in the success of your business. I firmly believe that is the best way to reduce the likelihood of loss and create a positive effect on our economy and our society.

ABOUT THE AUTHOR

Harry Clark is passionate about helping to educate and develop entrepreneurs. Through his breakthrough research, publications, speaking presentations, entrepreneurial risk-assessment survey, e-learning platforms, and blog, he hopes to make a difference in the entrepreneurial journey.

Harry founded Pathways Partners, LLC as a platform for business wealth creation and to educate and coach CEOs of private and public companies. He has more than thirty years of experience in a variety of industries, including management consulting, financial services, real estate development, construction, manufacturing, and consumer products.

He was formerly the CEO and co-founder of a $100-million modular design build and development company that served the educational and health-care markets. The company earned its ranking on the *Inc.* 500 list and was recognized as one of the fastest-growing, privately held companies in the United States.

Harry was also CEO and founder of the nation's leading municipal-finance-services firm. In this capacity, he was involved in 1,500 debt issues totaling in excess of two billion dollars. The company was ranked in the *Inc.* 500 and he was awarded Entrepreneur of the Year. He sold this company to MBIA, Inc., a *Fortune* 100 company.

After graduate school, he was a senior consultant for Deloitte Touche and Ernst & Young. He earned a bachelor of science and a master's degree in business administration from California State University, Long Beach, with international studies at the University of Copenhagen, Denmark.

Harry is a highly rated speaker on entrepreneurship, typically appearing before an audience that includes entrepreneurs, family business owners, and executives.